# Against the
# Catholic
# System

Professor Franco Cordero

Monsignor Carlo Colombo

# Against the
# Catholic
# System

## Franco Cordero

Translated with an
Introduction by

Anthony Johnson

Calder & Boyars

First published in Great Britain in 1972
by Calder & Boyars Ltd
18 Brewer Street London W1

Chapters 1-11 originally published in Italian as
Risposta a Monsignore by DeDonato

ISBN 0 7145 0936 1

Printed in Great Britain by
Biddles Ltd. Guildford

# CONTENTS

|   | Introduction | 7 |
|---|---|---|
|   | The Letter | 17 |
| I | Why Answer Back? | 19 |
| II | Thumbs Down Too Late | 27 |
| III | The White Genie | 29 |
| IV | My Sources | 38 |
| V | Theologian's Logic | 44 |
| VI | Sacraments and Magic | 53 |
| VII | Afraid to See | 59 |
| VIII | It's Better to be Blind | 66 |
| IX | Factory of the Faithful | 73 |
| X | The Good of the Young | 86 |
| XI | The Medicine of Terror | 95 |
|   | The Sequel | 106 |
|   | Notes | 128 |
|   | Biographical Information | 137 |
|   | Index | 138 |

# INTRODUCTION

On 1 February, 1970 L'Espresso published extracts
from Franco Cordero's Risposta a Monsignore (literally,
'Answer to Monsignor'), the book translated here as
Against the Catholic System.

Those extracts - two short columns - were enough.
'The truth, the whole truth and nothing but the truth'
was being told about an institution which had never been
talked about like this before - the Church in Italy.

Those few sentences put out deep roots in my mind
and two weeks later I heaved a heap of outstanding work
on to the shelves and wrote to Professor Cordero, to ask
if I could interview him. The result was published
in the Times Educational Supplement on 20 March:

Italy

PROFESSOR'S DISMISSAL REVEALS TENSIONS IN
ITALIAN SOCIETY

from Anthony Johnson

A small yellow paperback* brought out by the Italian
publisher De Donato has had the unusual achievement
(almost unique for a book so heavy with thought and
making no concessions whatsoever to 'popular taste') of
going into its third impression in three months - first
edition in January, second in February, and the third
this month.

The author, Franco Cordero, was born in 1928 at Cuneo, the Italian town halfway between Turin and Nice famous for 'never having produced a single Fascist'. He has been professor of criminal procedure at the Catholic University of Milan since 1960. In 1962 he was appointed professore incaricato (temporary professor) of the philosophy of law there, but lost this position in sensational circumstances last December.

In his stupendous flat in Milan, lavishly decorated with the canvases painted by his 11-year-old son and eight-year-old daughter (how many prodigies in the same family? I gulped), he told me that he had not sought this second professorship, but had, in fact, gone to some trouble to avoid getting it.

This was, he insisted, because right from the beginning he had foreseen difficulties. His method of teaching does not aim to be, or to make other people become, orthodox. It is that of actively inquiring into the subject in hand, independently of whether or not the results will turn out to be in line with orthodox beliefs.

Every appointment at the Catholic University has to be approved by a special theological commission. In the case of a 'temporary professorship' this happens annually. When, in 1967, Cordero published a book called Gli osservanti ('Practising Believers') he expected some kind of sharp reaction, because the book was based - I quote Monsignor Carlo Colombo, theological adviser to Pope Paul VI, writing his famous letter of criticism two years later - on 'a consistently held view of the holy life - a concept essential to Christianity - as a residue of belief in magic. Your method of juxtaposing authors and doctrines of different kinds (i.e., Catholic and non-Catholic) results in your treating them in substantially the same way. This operation is dubious from a scientific point of view and, as regards faith, is certainly corrosive.'

Monsignor Colombo's letter ended: 'As is my duty, I will inform the Rector and the Dean of the Faculty of the contents of this letter. But, because of the respect I feel for you, I am ready to hold a frank conversation with you when you like, I remember your family in my

8

prayers. '

When Gli osservanti first appeared, Cordero told me, there were mutterings in various places, but they were actually muffled by the Catholic authorities at the university. So, for the next academic year, 1968-69, he chose the book as a set text for the philosophy of law, and his lectures assumed a knowledge of it.

But then, instead of confirming his appointment as temporary professor in May last year, the faculty postponed their decision till July, then September and then December, as a 'crisis of scientific conscience' reached greater and greater proportions.

Then came the letter from Monsignor Colombo, to which Cordero's reply was the best-selling paperback. With immense, ruthless logic and incredible thoroughness, it probes into a hinterland of assumptions and implicit beliefs which, Cordero holds, lie behind Colombo's letter, and gives a point-by-point refutation of them. Invective of this sort hasn't been heard in Italy within living memory.

In a stormy faculty meeting in which his application for the renewal of his temporary professorship of the philosophy of law was turned down, the reason offered, Cordero told me, was that in Catholic university 'the aims of teaching must be in conformity with the principles of Catholicism whereas my starting point is that scientific principles can be separated from those of orthodoxy. '

Explaining his reasons for asking for the renewal of his position, Professor Cordero said, 'The fact that I attach no importance to holding my professorship of the philosophy of law can be seen from the contents of my latest books. But, faced with this recrudescence of bigoted repression, of the spirit of moral enslavement, and of the rejection of intelligence, I consider it my duty to apply for this post again, so that a decision, and the motives behind it, will have to come out, and so that everyone involved will have to give an account of themselves in public. '

In this quarrel, in the fact of Professor Cordero's

dismissal, and in the way he has been dismissed, many of the fundamental questions still eating away at the heart of Italian society have been raised. In the meantime no counter-reply has been formulated to Professor Cordero's 'Answer', and an eager public, thirsty for what will surely become a European classic of intellectual cut and thrust, goes on emptying the bookstores of a small yellow, pocket-size paperback.

*Risposta a Monsignore by Franco Cordero. No. 29 of series Dissensi (Voices of Dissent). De Donato, Bari. 600 lire.

An English-speaker on either side of the Atlantic might hastily conclude Cordero had a pyramid of chips on his shoulder and had been spiritedly shaking them off in a shower of rhetorical fireworks. This is decidedly not the case.

His analysis of this power hierarchy and its centuries-old methods goes so deep it stands as a compelling X-ray of any similar structure, sinking into the guts of the already fossilising state systems of Eastern Europe, of the 'we'll-absorb-you, give-and-take' British establishment and the less gentlemanly 'my-sword-in-your-back, yours-in-my-liver' gladiators' arena of American politics.

By now many people who refuse to identify themselves with their own national 'system' are willing to admit that the basic political problem is how to counter the de-humanising effects of a person-controlling hierarchy of power wielders. This challenges us with an intellectual task - to understand the system; and a practical one - to act against it.

It is no coincidence that Cordero is an Italian, a man who knows the Catholic circuit inside out, because this is the oldest, subtlest and most arrogant power system in the world, the only one which claims infallibility for its leader, which boasts of supernatural intervention to justify its most rapacious moves and which anathematises any form of opposition as sin (and therefore powered by diabolical forces).

His analysis of this most pretentious and experienced of all organisations takes the younger and more vigorous 'totalitarian churches' like Communism in its stride. As Simone Weil pointed out, when the Roman Empire absorbed Christianity, Christianity became an exercise in spiritual totalitarianism. And, even if the Church has been walking a bit groggily since the fall of Fascism in Italy - it was a natural enough counterpart on the temporal side to the claims to obedience exacted by the Pope on the spiritual (so much so that Mussolini got on very nicely with the Vatican, although he had started his career as a showy anti-cleric) - this hasn't been due to lack of power. The Democrazia Cristiana (Christian Democrat Party) has been in power continuously since 1948.

There is, I suspect, an inherent tension between the word 'Christian' (i.e. Catholic) and the word 'Democrat' in the expression 'Christian Democrat', just as - as Cordero points out - there is between 'Catholic' and 'University' in 'Catholic University'.

The Catholic Church in English-speaking countries has to some extent avoided the gaudiest vices of its parent, and many non-Catholics unthinkingly sentimentalise it. There are a number of reasons:

i. They really believe

The dilute-to-taste character of the Church of England produces the kind of nausea Christ described in 'Thou art neither hot nor cold, but lukewarm. Therefore will I spew thee out' - in uncompromising spirits. Often they go right ahead with Catholicism without ever realising that the central doctrine they are embracing commands the total submission of ideals to the concerted exercise of power.

ii. A united Church

Deep awe or a throb of admiration is produced in lay power-wielders by the thought of the sheer efficiency (in social and spiritual engineering of pliable human material)

of that well-oiled machine. One word from the Pope and
500 million people say yes; another from him, or his
successor, and 600 million people say no. Any ruthless
executive or politician will feel his mouth water at the
success of the operation; at the sheer effrontery of
unlimited power, like Tamburlaine:

> Is it not passing brave to be a king
> And ride in triumph through Persepolis?

or like the centurion who had (only) 100 men under him,
and 'When I say go they go, and when I say come they
come'.

They feel this without even realising fully, in most
cases, that this is the power-dream in its most refined
(but morally coarsest) form. The Pope giving his Christmas or Easter address is somehow holding a triumphal
dance on the heads of his worldwide flock, because he is
telling them what thoughts they must think, what acts
they must or must not do. The control is not exercised
(at least, directly) by firepower or fixed bayonets, but
is all the safer and surer for that. It is easier to smile
at the compulsory photo of Mao than at the calm, 'I'm
more cunning than you' smile of Paul VI, snapped as he
plans another move in the political game.

'United' in such a context means spineless, broken,
conditioned, done-for.

### iii. They're good Englishmen / Americans / ...like us

The feeling that these are loyal people, loyal to the
nation despite their blind, faces-flat-on-the-ground
allegiance to 'Christ's spokesman on earth' (or are all
the more capable of temporal loyalty because such ardent
practitioners of spiritual loyalty) makes an undeniable
impression.

English-speaking Catholics have generally fallen
over themselves backwards to prove that they are true
and loyal subjects.

Their being a minority has saved them from some
of the worst excesses of the Church in Italy, where
privilege and power (everything from ecclesiastical

companies paying no taxes, with up to twenty private cars
to a single executive, to legal smuggling by unstoppable
priests) has a single centre. Spiritual and political
intrigue are two arms of a single vortex.

### iv. A Catholic education is really something

Again, respect is produced by totalitarianism - in this
case applied to its most defenceless victims, the young.
The Catholic theory of education is based on the pre-
emptive strike. First, have as many children as your
wife can possibly bear. Second, ram your Catholicism
so deep home in them it'll never come out again.

'Get into a child's mind before it develops, or
before anyone else gets there'. Such a programme
(unbeatably totalitarian) is often announced in boastful,
enthusiastic tones by Catholics. The aggression is part
of the atmosphere, part of the dogma.

Overwhelming a child with total education (no half-
tones, all good and bad, either the Madonna or the Devil
behind everything) is made into an ideal. An education
which 'leaves its mark', which 'casts a person in an
unalterable mould'. Discipline is all. Everything down
to tones of voice and facial expression must be corrected.

Some people see this as parental responsibility.
They do not realise it leaves no child, only a monstrous
plaything or a battered, tormented, crushed rebel.

### v. They're R.C.. They're all right, I suppose

The typically Anglo-Saxon respect for 'the other side'
operates in religion too. Provided the 'rules of the game'
are respected, R.C.s fit into the usual, accepted culture
pattern. Any religious Brains Trust needs its R.C., a
bit bigoted, perhaps, but 'representing a point of view'.
With the difference that the other churches leave space
for personal thought and conviction, whereas an R.C. who
believes there is something personal about his conviction
is either inefficient or else nourishes a terrible illusion.
That member of the panel is there with less free play in
his mind than a Fascist thug or a Russian commissar.

## vi. Pope John was a sweet old man. It's a pity the present one isn't like him

Sentimentality is one of the chief and most noxious components of an average non-Catholic reaction. Stalin's 'paternalism' never cut much ice in English-speaking countries, and if Bill Stokes next door is a dear old fellow the thing stops there, but the combination of supreme power with some trace of humanity is enough to make many people (enough non-Catholics to fill St. Peter's Square many times over) go into ecstasies.

Perhaps they would like him to give a sweetie to the kids. Or to touch his papal robes. In any case, the thought that Pope John was a pleasant enough old man forces people to dwell on it, like a latter-day miracle. Without pausing to reflect that the fact that it is so strange is a macabre, sinister reflection of the 'corruption of absolute power'.

Would they really like Paul VI to have temporal power (as the Vatican so ardently desired till it was wrenched from it in 1870) or to dictate their every belief, in exchange for that sweetie?

The preceding remarks are intended simply to perforate the membrane of misunderstanding which inevitably separates two cultures as different as the Italian and the Anglo-Saxon. If the skin of the ecclesiastical apple looks clean and inviting, bite into it and see what a power-structure looks like at the core.

'If you understand a fact through and through, you understand a thousand others,' Cordero says. His remark can be applied to his own book, because his refusal to let spiritual coercion go unchallenged, however 'legitimised', 'sacred' or hardened by tradition, offers its own counter-ideology - 'rip ideas sacrilegiously to pieces and see what is inside' - a programme which can be applied any-where by anyone. 'The terrific destructive charge of philosophy, of Socrates, Galileo and Nietzsche, should be restored to it'.

I find this central concept of Cordero's more deeply

relevant to the twentieth-century conditon than those of the other authors who are really talking to us (and not only to a part of each of us or to some of us).

To mention a few names, taken slightly at random, Chomsky appears a shade amateurish and slipshod, however eager, after you've got Cordero into your system; Mailer, an adventurer in the psyche who fires at his targets, drunk, with a blunderbuss; Solzhenitsyn, a prisoner who wrenches his prison bars so hard they end up by closing us all in, without hope; Neruda, a romantic desperado, trying to knock back inhumanity with magnificent gestures; Voznesensky, a masterly exposer of injustice appealing to an audience whose skins are hardening faster than he can soften them.

Cordero handles the sciences without faltering - linguistic analysis, anthropology, psychology and sociology in particular, but handles them with the experience of a lawyer (he practised successfully for years), with the eye for detail of a professor of criminal procedure, and with the cunning and subtlety of a man brought up in the hardest school of Catholicism.

The realism he offers is exhilarating because it openmindedly accepts any situation and its dynamics. It leaves an indelible mark on the mind - the mark of a great author - especially because of the 'kickback' produced by its fierce-raiding logic, which instinctively heads for unexplored territory, so, incidentally, making some terrifying situations (terrifying because beyond human understanding) fit into a human dimension. And it is moral, because it forces the mind to a new consciousness of personal responsibility, in situations shown to be uniquely of our own making.

These, at least, are the impressions of a translator whose work has been a pleasure to himself, even before the publication of the book in English.

Postscript

A final word of warning. One possible reaction to Cordero's analysis (especially when he goes for the

central core of the system in the 1st two chapters) may be
'I can't believe it. The situation can't be that bad. I just
don't believe it's true'. Faced with such a reaction,
what can Cordero do? Show that he is telling a truth which
is part of the world, drawing an axis of experience into
which the religious sector of Italian life fits exactly?

The best evidence of all has been kindly supplied by
the Holy Congregation Pro Institutione Catholica (whose
spokesman is Cardinal Gabriele Maria Garrone), and
by the Vatican itself, in Documents A and C in 'The
Sequel' on pages 108 and 120 respectively. These documents should be pondered carefully. They are not 'freaks'
or 'mistakes'.

As to the human environment in which the system
operates, Cordero has written three novels, Genus,
Le masche and Opus. If the sceptical reader can't get
to Italy personally to do the necessary fieldwork, he or
she can at least read these when they come out in English.
In the world described here philosophically and
sociologically is given the tangible dimension of an
exhilarating nightmare-within-reality which reshapes
some basic ideas about the depths and heights open to
human nature.

Anthony Johnson

## THE LETTER

(written by Monsignor Carlo Colombo to Professor Cordero)

Dear Professor Cordero,

For some time - two years to be exact - some of my
friends had been telling me it was imperative that I should
read your book Gli osservanti (Practising Believers).
Unfortunately lack of time made this absolutely impossible.
A book like yours, written with the full commitment of
the author, requires an equally full commitment by the
reader; otherwise I would not have felt honest reading it.
And, although I have never allowed myself a holiday, I have
never succeeded in doing everything I should, at least,
not quickly.

In reading it I have tried to understand it as a book
of scientific research; in particular I have tried to
understand your method of enquiry, a phenomenological
one, guided, however, by clear personal convictions.
And I have, unfortunately, reached some painful conclusions. I do not wish to argue with your method, and,
above all, I admire your culture, which is really extra-
ordinarily deep. But I remain rather puzzled as to the
quality of your sources of information and culture. Your
book contains such a quantity of sources which are, let
us say, 'heterodox' - even where others were available -
that I have to doubt whether you have a deep knowledge of
Catholic doctrine or, in some cases, of Christian doctrine
in general. Above all I am struck by a repeated tendency
to bring up supposed contradictions between various
official dogmas and to put forward a constantly held view
of the holy life, a concept essential to Christianity, as a
residue of belief in magic. Your method of juxtaposing

authors and doctrines of different kinds, (i.e. Catholic and non-Catholic) results in your treating them in substantially the same way. This operation is dubious from a scientific point of view and, as regards faith, is certainly corrosive.

Quite candidly I must say I do not know how an intelligent young man who read your book carefully and understood it and the logic behind it could keep his Catholic faith, or, at least, how he could avoid finding himself in serious difficulties - difficulties against which you offer no effective help. It certainly seems to me he would find no help in making that comparison between Christian doctrine and lay culture which the bishops, in their communiqué last year, laid down as one of the characteristics of a Catholic university.

I am sure you will realise that, in writing the above, I have had a heavy heart. I have written after deep meditation and I have been thinking, above all, of the good of the young, as is my duty. It is also my duty to inform the Dean of the Faculty and the Rector of the contents of this letter. But, because of the respect I feel for you personally, I am ready to hold a frank conversation with you when you like. I remember you and your family in my prayers.

Very Reverend Monsignor,

Ordinarily letters like yours should not be answered.
Least of all in public. For 400 years now dogma has not
belonged to the domain of public discussion. All arguments
were squeezed to death when the Council of Trent sent out
its grim police to catalogue belief into do's and dont's. By
so doing it mummified theology.
　　The pedagogy of a closed society, the psychology of
faith, the anthropology of a human flock, and the sociology
of the church hierarchy...these are the only approach
roads left to a new understanding of the area of human
experience ruled by dogma. An analysis in terms of
'true or false' would bring a smile to the lips, and the
first to smile would be the most intelligent among you.
Anyway, your dogmatic assertions are so naively stated
that refuting them would be a dreadful mistake. Nothing
is as irritating as unnecessary refutation. 'When you
want to argue, choose a living target, not a stuffed dummy'
is a good motto.
　　Despite the risks, I must answer. You are a symbolic
figure. They call you 'The Pope's Theologian'. And I
can see by your modest smile that the rumour does not
upset you. It is generally believed that you played a part
in the sudden transformation scene produced by Humanae
Vitae. I wouldn't be surprised. There's nothing you like
more than oracular pronouncements. What must have
appealed to you most is that it condemned 'God's people'
to step up their reproduction rate so that the Church will
have plenty of docile raw material in its grip. And your

name crops up in all the secret reports on the worst acts of theological repression. Or so the authorities on the subject say.

A colleague of yours once called you 'an analytical mind'. This very churchy euphemism has a code meaning which can be deciphered roughly as follows - some people cannot be considered intelligent, as they are deaf to logic and have no imagination. But they are as painstaking and thorough as worker ants. And they have a knack of camouflaging their mental blank in sprays of words. This talent teeters towards cunning. These people have a natural leaning to detective-style intrigue. You have made your career by ferreting out suspect opinions.

It has been said that you have a penchant for getting caught out in unflattering situations. The facts are there all right, but I cannot accept the conclusions drawn by your critics. They are applying criteria which work in a shame culture. But the church is a guilt culture, and the criteria can't be rooted out of their sociological axes. Psychological optima are irrelevant to it.

I met you for the first time one day between Christmas '62 and the New Year. I didn't know much about you - a priest who taught theology at Venegono Seminary and was on the University Administrative Council - something like that. You were appointed bishop a year or two later.

Do you remember? You came late one afternoon, with a canvas suitcase and a manuscript. Sitting in armchairs we indulged in small talk. You favoured me with pleasant-sounding remarks, 'Fancy finding you here when everyone's on holiday'. I replied in the same style, wondering what you were driving at. What did I think of the tension within the university? You didn't like seeing people go for each other's throats. The remark betrayed an even-toned contempt for all factions. And what about the idea of holding a meeting of the whole university? No harm in talking things over a bit. The real purpose of your visit was, perhaps, to gauge what could be gained by 'cultivating my acquaintance', as you like to say.

A letter to you is a letter to the Catholic University of Milan, which you represent. You are the top religious authority in it. It is a formidable metropolis of university power - seven faculties, 20,000 students, state-recognised, a high-output factory of professors. People hope to get out of it a professional qualification which commands a financial premium, or a jumping-off position in the lower reaches of government. Universities, though, should be places where new ideas are formed through critical enquiry, and cultural values handed on. In the expression 'Catholic University' the adjective jars against the noun.

In some subjects the problem doesn't arise. Or you can at least pretend it doesn't. Criminal procedure, for instance, appears to fall outside the range of theological control. That's why I left Trieste University nine years ago to become Professor of Criminal Procedure here in Milan. I didn't have to pass any exams in orthodoxy, swear oaths of loyalty, go through initiation rites or be tattoed. If I had been told 'Every time you come up smack against a theological nerve-centre, you will have to bite your lip, calm your mind and say the theological tenet is scientifically true', I would never have come to the Catholic University at all.

These acts of acceptance entail a silent play of ambiguity. As new lecturers appear, they quietly drown the thought that some day they will be forced to choose between orthodoxy and intellectual self-respect. They think, 'The university authorities can't ask me to do or say something indefensible, can they?' So the assumption builds up that the authorities are tacitly waiving any claim to force them to assert what is intellectually untenable. 'Cardinal Bellarmino is dead now. Even the Church has developed a taste for intellectual freedom. No one is going to make me recant some scientific fact'.

A latent contradiction exists, but it may take a long time to mature, or may even resolve itself into a nearly institutional datum. Much depends on the mental level of the two sides. But due allowance must be made for the Realpolitik of the power struggle, the souring of professional resentment and the general orientation of Church policy. These are times of strong reactionary surges.

In my case, though, everything would have gone smoothly if the Faculty Council hadn't insisted on giving me the annually-renewable professorship of the philosophy of law in 1962. I had done my tactful best to steer clear of this unsolicited gift, because I could see it might make for trouble. The philosophy of law had for the previous thirty years been the feudal preserve of Don Olgiati, the most influential person at the University after Father Gemelli. Then things started getting very tricky.

In my first two years of teaching the philosophy of law, I based my course on logic and semantics. Even so, there was an area of friction with the old orthodoxy. Analysis of the Gothic dogmas of natural law was enough to arouse suspicion. After the first few minutes of analysis it becomes painfully clear that these dogmas are a jumble of ideas, or are meaningless. Or, if they have any meaning at all, it comes from experiences at a primitive tribal level.

Every new line of mental attack chafed the sore points. Then Gli osservanti was published. The affair dragged on for seven years, till the faculty, 'believing that the teaching of the philosophy of law in a Catholic University should be in conformity with the fundamental principles of Catholicism', concluded that my annual contract could not be renewed. They averred that my 'method... starts from a different premise, which is, that the philosophy of law can be taught independently of Catholic principles'.

This claim to subservience was a cultural anti-event of prime importance. The Catholic University of Milan stands round Piazza Sant'Ambrogio. What the Law Faculty did on 1 December 1969, with its vote for ortho-doxy, was to celebrate a funeral of science there.

A new classification of science subjects results. Do they come within the sphere of influence of theology, or not? Criminal procedure, for instance, can be taught at Catholic Universities as at other universities, even by non-Catholics. But in the philosophy of law something is only scientifically true if approved by dogma.

Scientific methods, as everyone knows, struggled

22

forward under ferocious oppression from the Church, in a no-man's-land where theology was unable to penetrate. Their postulate, which implicitly contradicted theological precepts, was that the world is a system of necessary phenomena. Forcibly introducing the whole range of theological idols, from 'acts of grace' to 'the Devil's tempters' into this neutral zone, would be to take a leap back into an animistic world. The 'accumulated wealth of revealed religion' would then give forth its edicts - Christian metaphysics dictating to philosophy, the dogma of original sin conditioning embryology, miracles a standing disproof of physics.

Some might object, 'Why shout scandal? There are philosophies to suit all tastes, from Plato and his ideals' to logical positivism. Everyone chooses their own marriage mate, party and religion. Cooped up in this philosophy, they contemplate the world through their chosen blinkers. Idealists, empiricists, the lot, they're all biased. The neo-Kantian world-view is no more ideologically shockproof than neo-Platonic fantasies. Varieties of Christian metaphysics are philosophies like the rest - not even the worst on the market. Why deny Thomists and Scotists the right to partisanship which you so liberally give lay philosophers? Let Catholics play about with philosophy as they like. '

This is a sly amalgam of two attitudes which have nothing in common. It's one thing to say you can't get out of your own skin or have two minds. Another to force others to think or at least speak in a certain way. The first is a biological fact, the second a normative expedient.

When I talk to my students about so-called 'natural law' my experience, which has crystallised into a set of mental habits, triggers off a whole series of tones of voice, of subtle inflections, of carefully weighed word-choices. Any barely attentive listeners realise I hold Don Olgiati's apologetics in no great esteem. But my conclusions emerge gradually from a controlled argument where the rules of the game have been respected. All my words have been given their accepted meanings - no underhand fiddling around - and the premises of the argument flow directly from facts which have the full backing of creditable scientific methods and can be double-checked. The conclusions run smoothly along the laws of inference. If anyone spots a mistake or thinks up better proofs, I admit it.

Dogmas, on the other hand, are road blocks on the way to thought. Discussions held under their auspices churn uselessly, because they are foolproof. No twinge of uncertainty, no shadow of risk. The beginning and end are known before you start.

The same kind of programmed-vs.-free polarity exists in law, between proofs which can be pondered by a judge and those which are legally binding. When a witness gives evidence, this presents many facets and no one can guess what the judge's conclusions will be. But with a legally valid confession he is bound to accept it, whether it is true or not.

But there is a difference too. The judge can openly admit that this is a legal convention he is bound to accept. No one need exclude a private view that what really happened was different. But a Catholic philosopher must accept the role of a cheat (if he accepts the principle of orthodoxy quoted above) because he has to assert that the dogma is scientifically true. His own views have to go in the ash can. Emotional conviction or charismatic revelation would be out of place.

One example may be enough to show where this principle leads. The Scholastics, theological pundits of the thirteenth century, re-varnishing a concept dear to the Stoics, held that the conscience is an organ of infallible moral intuition. Good and evil, therefore, are as rock-hard as mathematical quantities, as the terms in Pythagoras's equation. Shrewd observers, starting with the Sophists, guessed this wasn't exactly true. And now, with a mass of anthropological data available, it's clear that 'good' and 'evil' are variables which range within extremely wide limits. Linguistic analysis has uncovered the emotional jerk which releases a moral judgment. Psychoanalysis has revealed how the structure of the psyche is formed during these moments of decision.

Only the dead ashes of the old definition are left - assertions some people really believed were scientifically true 700 years ago.

How can a Catholic philosopher of law cope? My colleagues' ruling leaves no doubt. If he doesn't want to risk a trial or a spectacular disappearance, he must teach that we contain an organ of infallible moral judgment, called 'synderesis', and that moral values are objective, even if they have changed a little since good fathers sacrificed their eldest children to please God. Some thinkers have disagreed, but they were muddled or their minds were poisoned - the Sophists, Hobbes, Spinoza and the rest down to Sade, Nietzsche, Freud and Melanie Klein.

They were all wrong, St. Thomas Aquinas right. To get people to believe him, a Catholic must caricature his opponents' arguments or ignore them. The best policy of all is not to mention that they exist. On this topic - 'What is Conscience?' - the Catholic philosophy of law offers squeaky variations on themes in fashion in the thirteenth century. The facts which contradict them must be treated as if they didn't exist - large slices of anthropology, sociology, psychology and linguistic philosophy.

These are times, though, when ideas move around quickly. They cannot be hidden, especially if they are bulky. A special version of the past can't be cooked up for the needs of new initiates - some sources escape censorship. The best solution is to educate these new recruits so that they will themselves reject unorthodox thought.

This is not something out of Orwell, merely what happens every day. The faculty of law has now put it solemnly into rule form. As far as I know the only twentieth-century precedent is the cultural police run by Zhdanov in Stalin's Russia. But Lysenko at least felt he had to produce scientific arguments, even if they were bogus. Catholic censors are talking at a lower level. On their model, a university is a mass-production factory of partisan ignorance and intellectual malformation.

What looked at the beginning of this discussion like

a question about what is true has turned out to be a moral dilemma. I must decide. In some cases keeping quiet is the easiest, but most cowardly, solution. Worrying about the consequences is irrelevant. Things must take their course. The past teaches that nothing or hardly anything happens. The battle between integrity and coercion is an unresolved constant in social life. On one side religious feeling, moral passion, a reckless thirst for knowledge. On the other the inertia of a system straining to perpetuate itself. It sops up ideas and spews out formulae. And manufactures its totem-men, all alike, figurines in a magician's test-tube.

Luckily the system plays on level terms, or even at a disadvantage. It's like a soccer team trying to finish up with a draw, if possible a goal-less one. Although a ravenous absorber, it uses itself up a bit with every little effort. Besides, it has one weak point. Under its orders you see musicians, choristers, mimers, liturgists, consecrators, exorcisers, incense-bearers, confessors, homily-writers, holy water sprinklers, glossary-compilers, sorcerers, visionaries, stylites, faith-healers, fortune-tellers, jugglers, comforters, hired women mourners, euphemism-coiners, undertakers, reanimation experts, quacks, gluttons, beggars, alms-givers, excommunicators, apologists, canonists, theologians, fakers, pedagogues, libellers, heralds, hagiographers, exegetes, casuists, courtiers, singers, train-bearers, ladies' men, go-betweens, bankers, touts, shopkeepers, brokers, talent scouts, middlemen, plagiarists, slave-drivers, legis-lators, spies, bailiffs, guards, censors, cops, excisemen, hired killers, instructors, copy-downers, judges, com-promise-wanglers, warders, flagellators, executioners and their assistants - a limitless army. But even if it was ten times as big, it would be powerless when faced with an opportunity to stand on its own in the thin air of real freedom, like a tightrope walker. At least, that's how I understand the gospels.

'Dear Professor Cordero,

For some time - two years to be exact - some of my
friends had been telling me it was imperative that I
should read your book Gli osservanti.  Unfortunately
lack of time made this absolutely impossible.  A book
like yours, written with the full commitment of the
author, requires an equally full commitment by the
reader; otherwise I would not have felt honest reading
it.  And, although I have never allowed myself a holiday,
I have never succeeded in doing everything I should, at
least, not quickly. '

Gli osservanti ('Practising Believers') is a drill which
scoops up material from the subsoil of behavioural
controls - the whole range from neurotic rituals to
coroners' verdicts.  The aim is to find out what norms
are, what people think they are, and how they are
experienced.  Many age-old bits of doggerel morality
are given rough handling in it.  The effect on a Catholic
reader is traumatic - but the crisis ends in a selection.
Readers with moody, starchy minds get a mental short
circuit at the sight of someone rummaging under their
daily crust of belief.  A theatrical fit ends in a furious
reaction against the perpetrator of sacrilege.  But the
calmer ones, after the first moments of grim vertigo,
walk around with their eyes a bit further open.
        The world looks a different place.  Not half so bad
as the nightmare they were bludgeoned with under the
title 'unbelief'.  The false constellations of fairy lights

have been switched off. The phoney certainties go up in smoke. There are plenty of compensations too - for the first time things are seen as they really are. A network of never-explored relationships begins to surface. Deciphering the algebra of reality is a pleasure. The old measuring rods, good and evil, are seen now as states of mind. This does nothing to alter the fact that some things should be done, others not. But the criteria for our choices become our property and creation. They aren't part of an imaginary nature, or fables about revelation.

Truth, anyway, is a moral value in and by itself. And morality - a virile decision to manage your own life - is happy to use the rubble of shattered illusions to build on. Looking further down still, you see other abandoned things - the longing for the womb, the fear of emptiness, a need for comfort, and an expectation of future rewards. Pre-moral states of mind.

You can't imagine, Monsignor, how rewarding it is to hear students recounting their experience of being lost in those underground caves and then climbing up out of them. After the first few shocks one thought aloud, 'What's left, then, of all the old beliefs they taught us... the latest theology, for a start?' (Extraterrestrial depots of souls, rotas of rewards and punishments.) An already liberated priest answered 'Nothing. It's not worth talking about. It's all a lot of make-believe.'

At first sight your behaviour looks contradictory. You were forewarned about the explosive content of Gli osservanti, but allowed the book to circulate in complete freedom for two years. You might as well have let the whole thing ride. Real faith would have run no risks. But a condemnation arriving after two years looks stale. If I had been interested in gossip instead of ideas, I could have offered some convincing explanations for this strange behaviour.

'In reading it I have tried to understand it as a book of scientific research; in particular I have tried to understand your method of enquiry, a phenomenological one, guided, however, by clear personal convictions. And I have, unfortunately, reached some painful conclusions.'

Your first sentence here is loaded with the assumption that a theologian possesses a special key to abstract thought, while scientists have to scurry along at ground level, squeaking out inferior, banal messages.

It's only natural, I should have thought, that someone who reads a scientific book should try to understand it 'as' a scientific book. But the clue to your cryptic opening is the word 'phenomenological', which sounds as a warning call to all the rest. Even if your letter had stopped here, the condemnation would have been global, unreserved, irrevocable.

'Phenomenological' is a word to be pronounced with narrowed eyes and pursed lips. Phenomenologists work with the facts and ignore 'the rest'. Metaphysicians, on the other hand, skate over enchanted landscapes of pure essence. Two human types - burrowing mole, soaring lark.

Take an example. Laws emerge from society, and their lifespan depends on a diversity of factors - the state and structure of the economy, the relative strength of social classes, the dominant ideology, the nature of rising élites, the degree of respect enjoyed by church dignitaries, the intellectual climate and changes in it, and so on.

A Catholic philosopher of law brushes all this aside,
In his view a law is just or unjust, and therefore
'effective', or not, to the extent that it falls in line with
Catholic value-patterns. These might seem to stand
outside history, but are not so far outside that they can't
be manipulated by purple-mitred or Papal interpreters.
Any law in favour of birth-control would be inoperative,
juridically ineffective - 'what isn't just is not a law' (!)'
- just because the Pope pronounced against it in Humanae
Vitae. But the whole situation would be bindingly and
effectively reversed in law, in the twinkling of an eye,
once the Pope took better advice and pronounced the other
way.

I have been forced to use a few hazy expressions in
the last paragraph. These must now be analysed. What
does the 'binding effectiveness' of the law mean? On
examination it splits up, amoeba-wise, into two separate
meanings. It either means that I am very likely to get
punished, if I disobey it, by a body of men paid by the
ruling group to enforce it (that's what legal effectiveness
means) or that disobeying would mean going against the
behavioural norms chosen or uncritically accepted by the
society I've grown up in and which aims to condition me
(that's the meaning of moral duty).

The two ideas don't even touch. So there can be no
guarantee that my legal duty is my moral duty or vice
versa. Or even that one won't involve a violation of the
other.

You use a very convenient theory to fuse the two
ideas. (Non-Italians should note that it was expounded in
1940 Fascist-cum-authoritarian-Catholic Italy.) In theory,
you admit, legal and moral duty might clash. But in
practice this never or hardly ever happens[2]. Antigone,
who didn't have four centuries of Counter-Reformation
weighing on her, wouldn't have agreed.

My definitions in this discussion, please observe,
leave no gaps in my reasoning. Every word has its
precise meaning and together they create a context out of
which real situations emerge. A spasm runs through the
Catholic philosopher of law. No! he booms. Unjust laws

are not laws because they don't belong to the 'realm of justice'. So they cannot legally bind the citizen.

If the point is pressed home, 'What do you mean by this "binding effectiveness" of the law?' he will offer a tautology, 'I mean the property of all just laws'. And if you dare to take the final step and ask 'What is this property?', he will subside into injured resentment, while his mind throbs, 'What the devil is he trying to get at? It's so simple. Just ask your conscience. Anyway, what's all this quibbling about? To hell with logic!' Get any Catholic philosopher of law talking long enough and his philosophy goes bust.

Metaphysics is a time-saver for lazy thinkers. Digging into facts is a sweat. Building up a logical view of the world is equally hard on the brain. It demands unremitting concentration.

A metaphysician prods facts aside with the edge of his shoe. He doesn't approve. He's more at home in the galaxies of pure essence. An unmatched privilege. A handful of words like 'being', 'body', 'form' and 'essence' and he's away - building a skyscraper of thought out of nothing. These words are his fuel, like a spider's dribble. He can go on endlessly with his own spit.

The game will go on undisturbed till this carefree methodology of thought is challenged. People who award themselves diplomas in 'essence' hate the guts of the exact sciences. Logic demands clipped rhythms and lean expressions. At the first opportunity these people let themselves go, but after the fit is over, can't remember what they said. An interpreter would be needed, and is actually prescribed by St. Paul, for rites of pure sonic utterance made during mental rapture, 'Two or three people at most should speak, one after another and someone must interpret for them. If no interpreter is present, they shouldn't open their mouths during the meeting - everyone should speak to themselves only - or to God' (I Corinthians, 14, 27-29).

If someone gets down to analysing the speech of a metaphysician, distinguishing the passages that make sense from those that don't, it often turns out that a mass of nonsense has been spoken or else that the speaker has regressed to a primitive level of thought. When a believer in 'natural law' starts talking about the 'binding effectiveness of law' he is really imagining a potent fluid which emerges from the law and winds itself round the subject, forcing him or her to obey. Just laws give off the fluid; unjust ones don't. This venerated corner in the metaphysical market is really a swish version of mana[3].

Plato fed his imagination on a spellbinding dialectic, flinging the doors of philosophy wide open. After him, anyone could be a philosopher. Just follow Plato's infallible formula, occasional bouts of frenzy and unlimited linguistic freedom - the body is a prison, we are bound for the skies, 'Listen, the music of the spheres!', find immortality in me, the world is a game of shadows, look away from it to find reality, 'Do you know why some things are good, others beautiful, others true?' - 'Because, in the beyond, beyond where our senses reach, goodness, beauty and truth shine', 'Don't be duped by real events, we've got the essences here inside us', we'd never see the sun if it didn't have a solar nature; and plenty of adages of this blend which show someone's projective mechanisms have hijacked their mind.

Sitting like world-rulers on this vantage-point of thought, or, to be more exact, fantasy, the metaphysician is convinced he has an open-sesame key to all thought. He has his hands on 'the all' and can safely throw real details to the dogs. Instead of thinking, he dreams. Any logical skills, if he ever had them, go to rot. Without syntactical rigour as a backbone to his remarks, they disintegrate into spasms of desire.

The worst thing is, he revels in it. Like Odysseus's sailors, lording it with the lotus-eaters, he refuses to go back to the oars - in this case the tiresome business of pulling logic across a sea of experimental fact (the only kind of argument God accepts). He thinks other people can slave away at that - a fool's pastime. He's one of the elect. He has many traits in common with a savage drunk on magic - laziness, imagination in chaos, reasoning powers gone to seed, wishful thinking and low cunning. A caricature of intelligence. Men like that succumb to mental fatigue, but revive at the first opportunity to exercise their skill in cheating.

Reasoning with such people gets you nowhere. They will never stop exploiting powerful emotional urges. They can rely on a large measure of collusion from those under them and, as they are dedicated to the exercise of power, occupy an almost impregnable position. An anthropological revolution would be needed to oust them, so it's a safe bet that they will be there till the end of time.

It's not worth arguing with them. Logic is powerless against whimpers of desire and groans of ecstasy. If you ever coax one of them into an argument, fragments of dream world come drifting up. The two sides soon reach an impasse. The following is a rough model of what happens:

'It's getting dark. Let's turn on the light.'

'Provided the white genie agrees.'

'What's that?'

'The white genie? He who gives us light.'

'I don't follow. All I have to do is get up and switch on the light.'

'That's what you say. Light comes from him. The click of the switch is only a condition. We must go back to the real source, the genie.'

'Where is this genie? I can't see him.'

'Do you think reality is limited to what you see, then?'

'You can always find out about invisible things through their effects. Breathe a poisonous gas and you die.'

'Exactly. One of the white genie's effects is light. From his effect, light, we can go back to the first cause, the genie.'

'Why all this talk about genies when the electric light system explains everything?'

'If you're as stupid as that, I can't explain. Intuition is needed sometimes. You're very weak in that.'

'Intuition. I'd say it's a question of clear thinking.'

'The rationalist fanatic at work! Reason alone is

powerless. It's a pack animal, a drudge.'

'It works hard all right, but we can't do better till we get supernatural brain equipment. Use it properly, you can't do better than that. To hear you speak...'

'I can meet you on your own ground, you know. You want proofs based on fact. How do you prove the genie doesn't cause the light to go on? Where are your facts?'

'Now you ask me to prove you're wrong. I know I only have to turn the switch and the light comes on. I can prove it be experiment. The genie is your invention. If you want it taken seriously, offer some proofs. Otherwise you'd only have to talk and spirits, ghosts and leprechauns would crowd into the world as fast as the words came out of your mouth. Anyway, explain your choice. Why a white genie and not a black imp or an abominable snowman?'

'I don't like these paradoxes. You make experience into a fetish. You want everything proved by experiment. So how do you prove that theory - that theories are only true if proved experimentally?'

'You astonish me! The experimental principle is not a hypothesis. Without it we could never distinguish between fact and fantasy. But I was forgetting. A metaphysician like you has an immortal soul, which can do wonders even when the husk of the body has left it.'

'Sarcasm won't convince me. I think there's something seriously missing in you.'

'To make up for that, my brain works perfectly.'

'You're infatuated with the intellect. Mankind consists of more than logic. You would like to do without values and spiritual things. When I shut my eyes I see things of staggering beauty...'

'Excuse me, but it's getting late. I have a lecture to give at five. I'm paid for doing my work.'

'You sound envious. Why should I be ashamed of my success, if I deserve it? I must go too. My chauffeur's waiting. Monsignor's holding a meditation on the "Way of the Cross" at seven. I suppose you'll be going...'

'No, I'm afraid not.'

Many of you have never heard of Occam's razor, the principle that an argument should be cut down to the bare bones. The white genie is a symbol of all conceptual froth, from Plato's 'ideas' to the Scholastic forms. Why drag in 'the good' if morality can be explained with a few slices of psychology and sociology? The secrets of philosophy aren't a matter of sly bargaining. You must learn how to handle words well, accumulate a wealth of facts, and build arguments up logically so they click. Hegel's greatness lay in his power to absorb facts - everything from the Swedish alchemists to British electoral reform.

You think a licence to practise philosophy should be given to whoever masters a corpus of formulae taken from the thirteenth-century theologians. You might have the honesty to ask what practical problems they wanted to solve, instead of treating their writings like bits of a spell to be repeated out of context. You harp on 'the good' without ever wondering how such a phrase came into existence.

'The good' is a strange half-noun sired by the adjective 'good'. Originally 'good' meant 'with blue eyes and blond hair, skilful at setting traps and shooting arrows' - anyone could add to this definition. 'Good' reflects the interest of a group or tribe and is calculated to spark off a positive emotional response. 'The good' and 'goodness' are capsule words which can contain any number of specific ingredients.

Lepers have leprosy in common and healthy people health. Abstract nouns are a natural shorthand for general reference. You metaphysicians, though, stick to your vice of saying 'The good "comes before" good action', as if good actions wouldn't be good if they didn't have a high enough 'wattage of goodness' coming off them. Talk about 'universals' comes from a corner of the mind which has reverted to a primitive state.

A large skein of vested interests is at stake, though. So there should be no surprise at the strength of the resistance to killing off 'universals' and the like. The experimental principle and Occam's razor would make a clean sweep of your formulae, which serve as buttresses to the establishment.

Take the doctrine of transubstantiation. The moment a priest bless the bread and wine, they are supposed to turn into the body and blood of Christ through an instantaneous miracle in their 'substance' (metaphysical inner core) while their 'accidents' (real properties) are absolutely unchanged.

It once occurred to an open-minded theologian that after the advances made in atomic research, the language that could be used blandly 700 years ago looks a bit worn by now. If 'substance' is to be more than a blank label you can stick on anything, it should mean atoms, molecules and energy quanta.

You went for the man who said that. Interpreting transubstantiation in physical terms is 'not only a theological error, but a dangerous one'[4]. It's easy to see where the danger lies. As soon as the site of the alleged miracle has been identified, it turns out that the miracle was dreamed up by the theologians.

Your conclusions: transubstantiation is real but can never be tested experimentally, even in the future, because it affects the 'substance' which human senses can never get at. Thomas Aquinas had said that 'substance in itself is unknown to us, but is known through its accidents'[5]. Since then wine-making and testing have made great strides, but no contemporary theologian knows any more about the metaphysical properties of wine than his medieval counterparts many centuries ago[6]

The miracle is there, but it can never be seen by human eyes, on this earth anyway. It reminds me of the strange change which will come over the bodies of the elect when the last trumpet will sound and the most amazing invisible chemistry will take place[7].

Still, primitive people all enjoy talking about invisible things. Lévy-Bruhl gives stacks of examples.

Footnotes

1. Non erit lex quae justa non fuerit.

2. C. Colombo, 'Guerra e pace nel pensiero cristiano' ('War and Peace in Christian Thought') in Rivista di filosofia neoscolastica, 1940, p.265

3. Energy-force-power, the first abstract concept developed by primitive tribes. (Translator)

4. C. Colombo, Scritti teologici, Venegono, 1966, pp. 463, 485 f., 518

5. 'Secundum se est nobis ignota, innotescit autem per accidentia.'

6. Ibid., p.516

7. Ibid., p.469

'I do not wish to argue with your method, and, above all,
I admire your culture, which is really extraordinarily
deep. But I remain rather puzzled as to the quality of
your sources of information and culture. Your book
contains such a quantity of sources which are, let us
say, 'heterodox' - even where others were available -
that I have to doubt whether you have a deep knowledge
of Catholic doctrine or, in some cases, of Christian
doctrine in general.'

Your refusal to argue is not a declaration of neutrality.
The word 'phenomenological' was meant as a war-cry.
You don't object to specific phrases, but to a way of
thinking. Unearthing facts and turning over ideas are
acts of intolerable provocation to a régime which means
to keep its subjects in a state of severe mental anaemia.
    The system functions very well. It doesn't react to
differences in ideas, but when it encounters differences
in intellectual temperament even its least sensitive
feelers twitch. Its interest lies not in whether its
subjects underwrite this or that theory about the relationship between Father and Son or between the hierarchies
of angels (yesterday's dogma is today's heresy, and the
reverse) but in whether they are willing to accept each
new dogma as soon as it is issued by the Vatican experts.
    Orthodoxy means the capacity to follow every twist
and turn in official doctrine without the least flicker of
discomfort or interest in the debate. It's a kind of hypnosis
not without some agreeable sides to it.
    Moral selection operates in the same way. The

38

perpetrator of an underhand trick should not feel regret.
On the contrary. It increases the chances of a flowering
of grace, which requires a thick mulsh of sin. Actions
don't count. Thousands of them can be obliterated with
a single flare-up of repentance.

The essential quality is flexibility. This explains
why you prefer businessmen to ascetics any day. The
same mental set explains your distrust of religious
conviction (whereas the religious pornography of Mme.
Guyon and other women saints goes down very well).
After all, someone who has felt the shiver of discovery
cannot be kept on a lead afterwards. The ideal flock,
in your view, is a mass of devotees who leave theological
questions to the experts, are immune from dangers of
dionysiac excess, obey, sin just the right amount, and
think only the necessary minimum.

My culture attracts your suspicion because of the
'quality of my sources'. You find a crushing majority
'which are, let us say, "heterodox" - even where others
were available'. Realising you had ventured on dangerous
ground, you tried to tone down the effect by hedging
'heterodox' between inverted commas and adding 'let us
say'. All you achieved was to attract more attention to
what you had done.

The times are not ripe for theological terrorism
and caution is vital, but the Torquemada style comes
through like a dagger gleam. Only natural. The indig-
nation of people who accept blindfold a system which
commands complete obedience, and then feel queasy
about some of its necessary features, inspires little
confidence.

Freud is a heterodox source because, as an 'orthodox'
philosopher writes, he claims to 'extract gold from mud',
writes 'grotesquely', is 'indecent' and 'coarse'. He
ladles out an immoral therapy based on an anarchic
release of the instincts. Orthodox thought, by contrast,
gushes that 'mankind does not breathe death or unhappiness, but the oxygen of what is most deeply human and
grandiose in its nature as a spirit incarnate' (sic).

The same oracle proclaims that 'from this majestic height the bestial world of Freud disappears in the shadows and with it one of the gloomiest and most pessimistic views of human life''. In fact, you only have to take a look at Italian Catholics in business, politics or philosophy to see that they have been liberated from the slavery of animal drives. Some already twirl a halo round their head, others give off a strong smell of wild flowers, and others...

Marx is another offender. You were wise to avoid mentioning him by name. You can never be too sure what the future may hold. But if you could speak freely you would have words of fire for that shameful doctrine which sees human life, and religion too (!), as springing from an economic structure.

Darwin is an even worse criminal. His theory had disastrous repercussions on dogma. Not only did he shatter the Genesis account of creation, he also ruined the doctrine of original sin, based on the assumption of a single mating couple.

Copernicus, Kepler and Galileo are heterodox too, but you can't lay a finger on them. You must unctuously deplore the mistake made by the Holy Court three centuries ago. Stuff and nonsense, the Holy Court was right. When a system drags behind it the machinery of dogmas and institutions necessary to its monopoly of power, all hell is let loose if you allow the inquisitive to tamper with it. All the bits and pieces are interconnected. If you allow just one to be attacked - even at the least exposed point - the risk of total collapse is already imminent. Two Cardinals have criticised the new mass, deploring the 'desecration' of leaving out the names of two of the orders of angels. Once the rot starts with Seraphim, Cherubim, Thrones and Dominations, it will spread till even the presence of Christ in the Communion is in jeopardy. Then priests will lose their status as mediators between the human and the divine, and the Church will have lost its most useful spiritual jemmy.

Believe me, Monsignor, it's nonsense to divide sources into orthodox and 'let us say, "heterodox"'

ones. In science the word 'orthodox' isn't legal tender.
Scientific thought has always refused to pay toll dues to
theology for permission to move. Opinions are accepted
not because officially approved but because backed by a
reliable methodology of thought. Stigmatising the phenomenology of behavioural norms as 'heterodox' is not
one whit saner than trying to solve problems in infinitesimal
calculus or microbiology by reference to revealed religion.
As you know, 300 years ago your colleagues were figuring
out their astronomy from the Bible, instead of observing
the stars. In science, theories can only be called true,
false, or more or less probable, with reasons given.
Nothing else counts.

That overwhelming mass of 'let us say, "heterodox"'
sources leads you to suspect that I may not be fully informed as to 'Catholic doctrine or, in some cases...
Christian doctrine in general'. Let's get it straight. If
you are referring to things said and written below a
certain minimum level of competence, I don't mind
admitting they have only a marginal interest for me - as
documentary evidence of one way of thinking. But if by
'Catholic doctrine' you mean the canonical scriptures,
- the whole lot, from Genesis to the Apocalypse, plus
the history of dogma, a glance should have been enough
to warn you that I am armed to the teeth in this area.
Otherwise the bloodhounds of Catholicism would have
torn me limb from limb. Their mouths were watering.
The most painful thing in the leaden silence which
followed the publication of Gli osservanti was the anguish
of people whose words dry up on them and go dead.
    My book is dangerous - not to faith, but to the
establishment - because it strips down the mechanisms,
holds up the pieces and puts them together again. During
this process the mystique vanishes. One of the factors
which works most strongly in the régime's favour is that
laymen worry themselves stiff at the thought their analysis
may be incomplete. Coarse anti-clericalism can achieve
nothing because it is the child of intellectual vulgarity.
Enlightenment-style irony seems powerless when up

against an institution of this mass. And the wary lone investigator is nagged by the fear that he or she may not have probed right to the bottom - 'What if I've missed something? Or slipped up on a minor detail?' The fear of taking a total plunge, the mania about perfecting analysis before starting, results in paralysis.

If managed with cunning, the organisational apparatus of dogma can live peacefully off this yield of unasked-for submission due to the self-inhibitory urges outlined above. Anyway, there are usually strong feelings rooted in childhood hovering at the back of the mind and these reinforce the superstition that there is a residue of involuntary respect which cannot be spited.

As if that wasn't enough to guarantee church hierarchs an easy life, the theologians have spun an impenetrable wall of words round themselves. Even when a word is a flimsy husk round nothing, it has full status in a dictionary. In giving a name it seems that a new object has been brought into the world. Inventing a word is child's play, but getting rid of it afterwards takes a lot of sweating at logical analysis. The Scholastic doctrine of forms is an example.

St. Thomas said 'substantial forms in themselves are unknown to us, but they are known to us through their accidents i.e. properties [2].' If substantial forms only appear through their properties, why not talk about their properties and scrap the forms as irrelevant? 'Why use more when you can manage with less?' But it took four centuries, from Occam to Hume, before the concept of substance finally hit the bottom.

Even that's not all. The system can count on another resource, a style of logic you could call 'making your opponent drop'. Here's the trick. When there's a flagrant contradiction to be smuggled past the visitor's notice, he or she is forced to go on an exhausting verbal tramp, over acres of irrelevance or digression, so they can never fit the two contradictory items in the same mental vista. The theologians of the Counter-Reformation were eager to force a viable channel between Pelagian indeterminism and Luther's and Calvin's determinism, and worked like children blowing soap-bubbles, inventing endless series of middle terms, an obsessive pastime. If a conclusion would be too dangerous, a chain of reasoning must be left floating in mid-air...

## Footnotes

1. M. F. Sciacca, 'S. Freud e la psicoanalisi', in La filosofia oggi, Milan,
   La psicoanalisi nella cultura italiana, Turin, 1966, p. 121
2. Formae substantiales secundum se sunt nobis ignotae, innotescunt autem per accidentia.

'Above all I am struck by a repeated tendency to bring up
supposed contradictions between various official dogmas.'

Would you assert that the classified list of Catholic
dogmas can stand comparison with Euclid's Elements?
I thought it was general knowledge that most theological
work takes place in an area where logic has been blitzed
out of existence.  The clash between logic and dogma is
stale news.  To get deep in one, throttle the others.
Some people get their first impulse to plunge into
mysticism out of torturing themselves between them.

    Dogmas normally originate as a hardening-up pro-
cess over a silt of emotion or fantasy.  How could logic
get a foothold here?  If the ship of ecclesiastical power
is in danger of going down, how can issues like the
relationship between parts of a sentence get a serious
hearing?  Breaches in logic are a nominal price to pay
for the internal order of the Church.

    The guardians of orthodoxy have never worried
unduly about contradicting themselves when they are
fitting a bit in the mouth of some troublemaker.  The
growth of dogma derives not from self-indulgence in the
joys of theory, but from the practical needs of the
establishment.

    The doctrine of the Trinity is a classic example.  A
search through the first three gospels yields no trace of
it.  The creed of the first Christian community in Palestine fits into the scheme of the Jewish apocalypse: Jesus
is a Messiah, a man with fabulous talents who will found
the Kingdom of God on earth.  He had been killed, but had

come back to life and would reappear at any moment. The catch-phrase of the early Church, 'Maranatha!' means 'The Lord is coming!' Nothing else. Theology still hadn't taken root.

St. Paul was the innovator. Tormented by an over-burdened imagination - so much so that many of his ideas went over his listeners' heads and never got taken in properly - he threw the Judaic 'Messiah' out. He had to give his message wider resonance, so it could strike deep roots in the living tissue of Mediterranean culture.

Paul introduced a new figure, whose philosophical counterpart was 'Logos', 'the word' in the theories of the Alexandrian school. A two-way interpreter, a mediator, a middleman between God and man - capable of rounding off the work of creation too. He had to be a divinity of slightly inferior rank.

The relationship between God and this figure was never clearly defined. The first was simply God and there was no other. The second acted as his long arm and was 'the first born of creation'. With equal pro-priety he could be called 'Kyrios', 'Lord' or 'Christ' - the Greek word for anointed, retranslateable as 'Messiah' in Hebrew. The Greek model of a pre-existing divine being (a second rank divinity) absorbed the Judaic one of a man chosen as Viceroy of God on earth.

But Paul was less interested in the family trees of divinities than in the future of the human race. Paul had made Jesus a half-divinity, but he gave him another role too, 'Saviour', another figure from the Greek cupboard. Orpheus too had been both Lord and Saviour (the word 'Saviour' was used as a personal name by the House of Ptolemy in Egypt). Christ had saved mankind by be-coming flesh, being crucified and rising again. He had to save mankind from the corruption caused by Adam eating the apple.

At this point Paul brought the myth of Anthropos into play, with the dialectic between the 'two Adams' - one bad (carnal), the other good (spiritual). In a gambit typical of primitive thought, each Adam had to compress the whole of the human race into himself.

The death and resurrection of Christ have unleashed a cosmic revolution, freeing cataracts of 'pneumatic' energy. To capture this a mysterious rite is needed - baptism. Each believer must re-enact in his or her own body the death and resurrection of Christ. Death becomes immersion in water, - resurrection, emersion. This ceremonial grafts the believer on to the 'mystic body' or corpus of believers that has formed round the Lord. That is what Paul meant by 'in Christ', a phrase he repeats in his letters with obsessive frequency.

The third divinity, the Spirit, still had no clear identity. The word spirit, which corresponds to mana, orenda, bráhman, and others, refers to the invisible active agent in any abnormal event, from epilepsy to the enthusiasm of a thiasos. The first references to it appear in the fourth gospel, where it is called 'counsellor' or 'paraclete'. After Christ had left earth for Heaven, the Spirit had taken his place, to distribute a non-stop revelation. But the doctrine of the Trinity still hadn't been mooted.

In any case, Christianity during its first 200 years was a cauldron with thousands of ingredients swirling round in it. It was anyone's guess which would prevail.

The Gnostics jettisoned the Old Testament, had a pessimistic world view, and denied that Christ had been human. It was objected that this made salvation impossible. A middle term, a man-plus-God rolled into one, was needed to jack mankind up to the level of God. In the meantime Christianity had been absorbing the Greek idea of spiritual regeneration. An initiate saved himself by becoming one with a heavenly partner. Christ or Logos had to be the catalyst in this transmutation.

Christ was supposed to have been generated by God - to have emanated from him. But how can his God-like features be reconciled with the one-god motif annexed from Judaism? The only logical answer is that Father, Son, and, if necessary, Spirit, are personae, masks, for a single God. Remaining always the same, he would then appear sometimes as Creator, sometimes as Saviour and sometimes as Counsellor. His name would change accordingly. That was the nucleus of the Sabellian heresy.

The majority faction objected that if this was true, the Father must have died on the cross. Impossible. There must be a real difference between the three, not a difference of names. But this meant two Gods, at least, unless Christ was demoted. Origen said the Son is eternally generated by the Father - is an 'image' of him 'just as radiance is generated by light' ', but is also a hypostasis or separate being. Back to square one.

This vexed question blew up violently in the fourth century, as soon as Arius mapped out an obvious con- clusion. If the Son was generated by the Father, there must have been a time when there was no Son. Besides, they couldn't share the same essence. So the Son was not God. Anyone who disagreed must believe in more than one God. A faultless argument, but the Bishop of Alexandria (Arius was one of his presbyters) shrieked out an alarm against heresy. Pandemonium ensued.

The Emperor Constantine needed a united Church under him. He summoned the Nicene Council, the first in the history of the Church. The minority faction led by Arius had to be outlawed. If it had been bigger the Nicene creed would have been Arian instead. The law of numbers decided the issue. That is why the Son is called 'Light from light, true God from true God, begotten not made, of one substance with the Father'. Mere juggling with words.

The adjective homousios used to seal the identity of essence of Father and Son seemed to many to have a whiff of the Sabellian heresy about it. But when Con- stantine let it be known that he liked it, all opposition crumbled. ('Render to Caesar...')

Then Eusebius of Nicomedia replaced Osius of Cordoba as the Emperor's theologian. The tables were turned - Arius came back from exile, Athanasius, leader of the Nicean faction, went into it. The Arians were rehabilitated. Emperor Constans I summoned Councils at Rimini, for the West, and Seleucia, for the East. The losing line at Nicea now had a majority.

At Nicea Constantine had tried to end the argument

by crushing the weaker faction. At Rimini and Seleucia the tactic was to snuff the debate out by concocting a formula which would suit the ears of both parties. After all, the Scriptures gave no verdict as to whether the Son was homousios vis-à-vis the Father, or, for that matter, any inkling of the relationships between the three Persons. The wisest move was to close the discussion. The Council voted an ambiguous motion and withdrew the controversial terms from circulation.

Under Theodosius, however, the Athanasian faction got the upper hand again. The Council of Constantinople restored the Nicene creed. God was once again one in three persons ('person' here not as 'mask' but as or individual), three eternal equals. The dogma of the Trinity had finally made it. The definition is pitiable, but they couldn't find a better one. Besides, both parties were flat out. Every problem has its genesis, growth and death. By now the problem of the Trinity had lost all the fizz it ever contained. Exhaustion was decisive.

The question slept for eleven centuries (except for Abelard's indiscretions). It was unearthed by the Italian heretics of the sixteenth century, incited by their philological interests (Lorenzo Valla's analysis of the word persona). This episode was a landmark in Italian culture, but left almost no trace in the history of the Church.

Since then no mention of the subject. There's everything to be lost, Monsignor, by injecting life into it now. When talking about it, all thoughts of logic should be left in the lobby, a mental blank must snap down like à visor, and the authorised text be repeated word for word without ever faltering from the standardised orchestral drone - the Father eternally begets the Son, the Son is eternally begotten and the Holy Spirit proceeds from both.

I hope you have enjoyed this sample of the phenomenological method. A short trip behind the scenes, and the gestation of the dogma of the Trinity slips easily into focus. What went into it?

A strong emotion (Christ worshipped as deity)
A religious precedent (the Judaic belief in one God)
A logical dilemma (how to reconcile Christ's divinity
with the one-God principle)
Two Greek ideas: Logos (in Philo's sense);
The idea of the Spirit proceeding
or radiating from Father and Son
(in Origen's sense)
The antagonistic furore of theological warfare, with
its inevitable ant-heap of individual ambitions
The crafty chemistry of the political game
Court intrigues
The needs of authority
The subtlety of compromise
The progressive exhaustion of two factions
The final conclusion that rickety compromise was
preferable to permanent brawl.

With this background how can dogma help being an insult
to logic? Its purpose at the moment of proclamation is
usually to act as a sedative against a dangerous squabble
- a solution on the Rimini-Seleucia model (not the Nicene
one), incorporating unresolved contradictions in a
meaningless text. A decision one way or the other
would mean losing the minority faction, and amputations
of this kind leave a stiff bill to be paid.

The best policy is to weave a web of words where
both sides recognise their own ideas. And trust to the
anaesthetic properties of time.

Another classic example is the cross-fire of diatribes over grace. Are we masters of our actions or
does God jog our elbows? The Council of Trent said
'Yes, both'.

This practice of deliberately blanketing out logical
fires softens up people's brains. It weakens or destroys
their awareness of logical contradiction. Besides, the
situation gets grimmer. The experts develop a knack
for creating complications. A criminal caricature of
logic. Treatises on grace seethe with these cats' cradles
of words which lead nowhere.

The disease affects morality too. Clear ideas and moral rectitude usually go together. The same delight in order presides over both. Turgid thinkers, on the other hand, have a natural bent for moral incoherence, if for no other reason than that it allows them to pursue the worst perversions without leaving the least slick of conscience on their minds. Behaviour based on starving intelligence and forcing logic off its hinges rapidly degenerates into moral anaesthesia or foxy careerism.

How do you see the theologian's work? Your ideal is the metodo regressivo - the regressive method. You say it without a shade of irony. We must consider the teachings of the Magisterium ('leading' authorities in the Church) to be unalloyed gold, and follow the traditions back in time to their source, to find - as we must - that they originate in the Scriptures [2].

Revelation came to a full stop on the cross with Christ and no additions are permitted. The scriptures contain the complete range of truths, but some are there only in embryo. Dogmas must be enunciated to make explicit what was only implicit. In latent form they were present from first to last in the apostles' minds. Their understanding of revelation was an unrepeatable climax. The trouble is...they didn't know it. But if someone had asked them, the perfect answer would have spurted to their lips [3] (without the intervention of 'authority').

The post-apostolic church has had to make do with a lower variety of knowledge. But there's no need to panic - the Holy Ghost takes the strain. The verdicts of the leading authorities are infallible, independently of the moral and intellectual standing of the men who mouth them [4].

The growth of dogma is a 'supernatural historical fact'- something to take on trust, in other words. That doesn't mean it cannot be 'proved by valid arguments' [5] that the Holy Ghost had a hand in it, even if you, in your writings, apparently had no time or space to air them. Arguments or no arguments, though, analysis of the genesis of dogma has to admit defeat when confronted by an inscrutable residue - the supernatural factor - visible only to theological eyes [6].

A 'real contradiction' between history and theology is impossible as long as history respects 'theology's legitimate autonomy in methods and conclusions'. No historiographer can arrogate to himself the right to cast doubt on an event which 'theological principles show did necessarily happen'[7] just because he cannot track down the least evidence of it, or because it is a physical impossibility - the taking of Mary into Heaven, for instance.

Why use scientific methods at all in historiography, then? To confute 'historical reconstructions out of line with dogmatic principles'. To put it kindly, science is tolerated as long as it serves your turn, but the moment it produces inconvenient facts, must be shown the door. The final touch is your assertion the history of dogma [8] itself proves that 'God has wanted the knowledge of revelation to grow'[9].

The scriptures contain the A to Z of dogma, but some of it is only implicit. How many latent truths have yet to be revealed? Er...we'll only know that at the end of time, because Holy Mother is a tireless worker, and no one can guess how many more cards she has up her sleeve.

All the same, there must be some connection between explicitly revealed truths and truths discovered later, otherwise (Holy Ghost apart) the specialists of the Magisterium could go on pulling infallible truths out of their heads as fast as the ideas rolled in. Yes, indeed, there must be, but we must be content if it is visible to the faithful[10]. You must be visited by grace to understand revealed truths[11].

The taking of Mary into Heaven is a good example. The scriptures say nothing about this. Nor do they say that she was immaculately conceived (sine labe originali) but both dogmas have pride of place in Catholic thought.

When the Church authorities force believers to subscribe to a dogma and you cannot see where they got it from, the only possible solution is that it was publicly revealed before the death of the last apostle, or that the dogma is somehow incorporated in the scriptures, whether visible there or not. A Catholic can let his mind thresh about a bit, but there is no escape from this dilemma. The Immaculate Conception and the Assumption of Mary into Heaven must be believed to be part of the canonical texts, although, if you search them all, from Genesis to the Apocalypse, you cannot find a syllable about them[12]. The 'regressive method' must work miracles.

I acknowledge that you have a special flair for Mariology. A devastating passage compares the Madonna with Queen Astrid of Belgium. She too influences 'her subjects with the glamour of her personality'[13].

Perhaps turning the argument towards the clash between logic and dogma was not such a good idea.

## Footnotes

1. 'Sicut splendor generatur a luce.'
2. Scritti teologici, pp. 44f., 127, 135f.
3. Ibid., p. 109
4. Ibid., p. 115
5. Ibid., p. 123
6. Ibid., p. 124 f.
7. Ibid., p. 126 . Earlier (p. 42) the point is put like this - 'The certain teaching of the leading Church authorities is an externally-operative prohibitive norm for the study of history as for any other kind of scientific research'.
8. Ibid., p. 127
9. Ibid., p. 135
10. Ibid., p. 100 f.
11. Ibid., p. 106
12. Ibid., p. 337 f. and p. 353
13. Ibid., p. 405

'...and to put forward a constantly held view of the
sacramental life - a concept essential to Christianity -
as a residue of belief in magic.'

You oversimplify. The word 'magic' is generally used
in such contexts to imply contempt, and has a vague
meaning. I used it in a clear and emotionally neutral
sense, to describe some of the dogmatically uncontro-
versial aspects of the sacraments. And I gave my
sources, from Peter Lombard to the decrees of the
Council of Trent.

Once this is agreed, you would either have to reject
my description as inaccurate, or limit your disagreement to an aesthetic preference for another word of
identical meaning, saying 'Your description is correct,
but I object to the use of the word "magic" in this connection. Here's how I want it used...'

You do neither. You don't deny my theological
premises or say you prefer to use 'magic' in other
contexts. So your disagreement flaps in a void. Turn
the phrase round as often as you like, but it boils down
to the accusation that I see something magical in 'the
sacramental life - a concept essential to Christianity'.

Apart from the glaring inaccuracy (Zwingli, for
instance, did not accept the Communion, but has never,
as far as I know, been accused of not being a Christian),
this is not an argument at all. Ritual murder was
'essential to the religious life' of the Aztecs, and holy
prostitution to that of the Phoenician towns. If judgments
on value had to be based on the need felt for things,

drugs would win the contest, because addicts cannot face
life without their daily dose of dope.

I will tackle the question of the sacraments where
the arguments have always started, the Communion. To
understand its origin, you have only to form a clear
image of the scene when the early Christian communities
in Palestine made dining a rite. In commemorating the
last supper, mysterious things began to happen. The
air became heavy with longing, 'The Lord is coming!
(the thought in every mind) till desire redoubled within
the closed crucible of the group (each celebrant mirroring
his or her own feelings in the others) till an overpowering
impression was produced that Christ was really coming.
Had come! 'The Lord is here, is with us!' grew into a
conviction, and the commemoration dinner turned into a
Messianic feast. The quantum jump from individual
anguish to collective mesmerism is the true origin of
the divine-presence Communion.

Then the rite took on a Greek softness along a line
of development reflected in the sacramental theology of
St. John's gospel. The unbearable tension of waiting for
Christ dropped. Judaic realism receded. The eerie
half-shades of a fleshless other-world began to predominate. Initiates rolled themselves in the music of
words like 'Christ', 'light', 'holy', 'immortality'.
Salvation meant superseding the human condition - be-
coming transhuman - and the sacraments were the way
to crash the barrier, the Christian version of the Mediterranean mysteries. The Communion, in particular,
offered nourishment for a spiritual life which was already
deeply embedded in the Greek sensibility.

The sacraments presuppose a solid or liquid of
supernatural potency which, however, can only be transmitted by touch. The only substance originally imbued
with this power was Christ's blood 'one drop of which' a
hymn by St. Thomas tells us 'can purify the entire world
of all its sins'. Marlowe's Faust took a similar line:

> See, see, where Christ's blood streams in the firmament!
> One drop would save my soul - half a drop: ah, my Christ!

A flood of 'pneumatic' energy must have broken away from the body on the cross and spread over the earth's crust. When one of the soldiers plunged his sword into Christ's side, blood and water spurted out together[1] . 'The sacraments on which the Church is built flow from the ribs of Christ, so the potency of the Passion lives on in the sacraments given by the Church'[2] .

To get back to the Communion. Saying mass requires an initiate. The same words and gestures from a layman have no effect. Supernatural power is needed, and priests monopolise it. It was transmitted to each by the laying on of hands by another such initiate. The key moment in ordination is when the ordaining priest's hands settle on the new priest's head. That is when he lets his mana flow into the new priest. A carbon-chain sequence of ordinations runs back uninterruptedly to the Apostles, whose powers came from the touch of Christ.

Like all those whose profession is power, a priest has to accept various taboos. He is required to lead a life of segregation and avoid 'laying hands' on women. Ordination leaves an indelible imprint on him. Unfrocked priests retain their powers and must not use them.

The Communion consists essentially of a motto and a gesture. These are used to bless the bread and wine, so transmuting their 'substance' into the body and blood of Christ, without even grazing their properties or 'accidents'. Johannes Teutonicus is said to have held mass simultaneously in Halberstadt, Mainz and Cologne - an amazing feat. But can it really be compared with what a priest achieves when he blesses bread and wine?

Despite the miracle, not the least effort is involved. The priest doesn't have to hold himself at full stretch, like a bow strung to breaking point the moment before the arrow twangs away. The miracle never fails even if he stammers or gesticulates wildly, with his mind miles away. It is all the more impressive in this case, because independent of its author's skill. Saint or lecher, ascetic or drunkard, model of chastity or crack seducer, he works the miracle. His behaviour is not superhuman. On the contrary, it is supposed to be a sequence of words and movements which automatically trigger off their effects like clockwork, a prototype for the twentieth-century idée fixe of a finger pushing a button to start a world war.

But here the performance is far more spectacular, though completely invisible. It can be felt, however, and when a believer soaks his wafer on his tongue, he is conscious of a mystic presence.

This is a double event, theologians say. First there is the so-called 'indwelling' of the Holy Spirit or the whole Trinity, who lodge in the soul as its guests[3]. Second, an impersonal fluid runs through the believer, 'something supernatural going from God to man'[4], so-called 'created grace', which Aquinas calls 'a quantity of the soul'[5].

But if the communicant is a sacrilegious heretic - or even a thick-skinned believer, the softening of the wafer is no more than the movement and suction of tongue against palate, like a musical phrase rebounding uselessly off a deaf man's ears. A mischievous spectator might suggest that the effect is psychological, not metaphysical at all. But remarks in this style draw no response.

In describing the Communion, I have concentrated on isolating its features, to aid in its classification. This is not to exclude the invisible side. For all you or I know, blessing bread and wine really does produce a sure-fire miracle. How could anyone prove it doesn't, if invisible effects cannot, by definition, be traced? If, however, we have found all the characteristics of magic in this rite, why refuse to admit that magic is being practised?

The metaphysicians of your school may still believe in 'universals', but everyone else realises by now that verbal classification is arbitrary. Here I am using the word 'magic' to mean actions, usually performed by a qualified expert, which aim to change things in this or another world through a network of cause and effect which cannot be checked experimentally.

Psychologists state that this cult of 'an expertise of

change' is due to a desire to 'make thought all-powerful'. The officiating expert wishes his wish, adds a few frills of ritual, and out comes the result. The theoretical implications are fairly complex. So defined, magic requires an extremely powerful strain of energy, able to move at lightning speed between things in contact or of similar appearance.

How can the priest's actions at mass be excluded from such a definition? If the classification is dispassionate, there is nothing irreverent about saying so, either. From this standpoint, baptism is on the same level as bull-cults, spells and fertility rites.

A reader of Mauss[6] might protest that the sacraments are part of the religious life, which is public and congregational, whereas magic is typically a night-time affair, surrounded by mystery and furtiveness. 'Quite true,' I'd agree, 'but such factors are only relevant from a social angle. Which falls outside my definition.'

Everyone is more or less conscious of the truth of what I have said in this chapter. I imagine you wouldn't agree to freely debate the question of ecclesiastical celibacy. Have you ever wondered why? Isn't it because anyone whose profession is the supernatural has to pay the price of a taboo against sexual indulgence. This is a standard feature of the mystique of magic. Ecclesiastical celibacy and sacramental magic stand and fall together. The Reformation shows that when the magic is abolished, the celibacy is too.

Difficult black magic calls for a properly ordained priest. The plus sign turns to minus, white to black, but the operation is the same. Mana is a fluid which comes in two colours. So does the spirit of God - as the Pharaoh learnt to his cost. First God hardened his heart, then punished him for it.

Footnotes

1. John, 19, 34
2. St. Thomas, Summa Theologiae, 3a Suppl., 17, 1, c.
3. C. Colombo, De Gratia, Venegono, 1956, 112 f.

4. 'Quiddam supernaturale in homine a Deo proveniens', St. Thomas, Summa Theologiae, 1a - 2ae, 110, 1, c.
5. 'Qualitas animae', Ibid. , 110, 2, c.
6. M. Mauss, Teoria Generale della magia, Turin, 1965, p. 89

'Your method of juxtaposing authors and doctrines of different kinds, (i.e. Catholic and non-Catholic) results in your treating them in substantially the same way. This operation is dubious from a scientific point of view and, as regards faith, is certainly corrosive.'

What frightens you about my book? It shows things without masks, thick ones and thin, big and small, sharp and blunt, long and short, nice-smelling and evil-smelling. Things just as they are before an improving mind gets to work on them, with eyes to tear off unwanted material and hands to manipulate censorial scissors, to tart up the end-product with daubs of sentiment. That is how you turn everything to a stereotype, and occasionally slip disastrously down a crevasse of total evasion.

It must be infuriating to see things unadorned, without the rouge, lipstick and chocolate-box frills which you judge to be necessary before facts can appear on the stage of public or even private attention. Damned facts might at least freeze in one position or let themselves be seen from a distance. But they stand naked in my book, as large as life, and moving disturbingly, revealing hidden relationships you had never had the misfortune to be forced to see before.

The woof of the world is different from what anyone would swear it to be without looking at it. Every fact connects up with every other. Look at the 'highest' or 'noblest' and you can always find a direct route to the 'lowest' or 'basest'. Incredible, maybe, but true.

Understand a situation through and through and you understand a thousand others. The arts of courtship, child labour in textile mills, saying the evening rosary - there you have three different worlds, each full of meaning. After you have undone the machinery in each, down to the last nut and bolt, and reassembled them, you have understood a great deal about human existence. A knowledge ranging from theories of beauty to what stimulates an economy.

All in the same family tree! Nothing escapes: sex and St. Marguerite Marie Alacoque; cannibalism and devouring Christ at mass; sacrificing the firstborn and dedication to the Sacred Heart of Jesus; maximising profit margins and rewards accruing in the safes of Heaven; the cut-throat mentality and theological rapier-thrusts; drowning children with irregular teeth and the Index of Prohibited Books; exhibitionism and moral asceticism.

The spiral widens along a line of unforeseen analogies. Absolute values and unbending hierarchies fall, chopped down by the sword of logic. Cushioned walls and reinforced bulkheads crash. You find yourself at the centre of an awe-inspiring whirlwind of objects, set out in splendid constellations, breaking up and coming together again against a horizon of limitless, deaf, amorphous fact'.

The seething ant-heap of sense-impressions yields no truce, and erodes the defence mechanisms like high-strength acid. The eyes are open with a new intention. The best way of dismantling an 'innate idea' is to show how it was made - workbench, glue and all.

The primordial disaster, it transpires, was deciding to live in a castle of set verbal models. There's no shortage of people who wouldn't know how to live without such a verbal stronghold. But their sacred cows of thought, from the six-day creation to that decisive couple Adam and Eve and on to the concentric shells of the Heavenly Spheres, stare glassily and stupidly at the ever-changing mesh of reality. A trauma. The mind must start all over again, even at the risk of losing its own identity, or be forced to negate facts at every step.

The Catholic Church has always been a masterly practitioner of this second solution, but for some time now has been shy about admitting it. It aims to whip out of the mind, or, better still, never allow in, any fact which could disturb the tramping-board of emotional equilibrium.

But this repression exacts its own price. The still-born material wanders around disconsolately in the underworld of the psyche, thrusting up against its crust, trying to find a way up.

At key points an eruption is possible. The psyche itself identifies them and installs its devices, 'symptoms' and compulsive behaviour. At intervals the patient blurts out some apparently inexplicable remark, or goes berserk, acting on an irresistible impulse.

Your attitude reveals a mental state so common I would like to analyse its origins by focusing on a crucial phase in European history, 1100-1300, a period of often overwhelming intellectual temptations. Consider the life-style of the previous century. The world was like a gigantic church. The horizon didn't stretch far - its radius was confined to the ingredients necessary to spiritual salvation. The only exception was the minute residue of Platonism and neo-Platonism which had seeped into the practical mind of St. Augustine. Only one science was tolerated - Bible-study - and it had few books on its worktable. Where this world stopped the next began. Like the furious sea raging beyond the Pillars of Hercules, the air pullulated with angels and demons, saints and fiends.

When the soul is at stake practical interests immediately predominate. The society which harboured this mental parasitism rotted. Compared with eleventh-century Europe, the Jews and Arabs could each boast a society of dazzling brilliance. The Cordoba Mosque with its algebraic frenzy is a tight-rope walk across space by pure intelligence. Compared with that, Gothic churches' progress to Heaven is monolithic, club-footed, pug nosed, squat, overloaded, grey.

Roused by these intellectually advanced societies tapping at its shoulders, the West finally became interested in reality. The shock was violent, and (as always happens) it brought with it a premium of interest in theory. The other world looks nice, but we aren't there yet. Let's have a look at this one in the meantime. In philosophy the dam broke when Aristotle was rediscovered, re-routed through the Arab commentators. The Augustinian tradition shrivelled. We're sick of hearing about essences which exist only God knows where. People wanted to talk about what they could see, hear, feel, taste and smell.

St. Thomas Aquinas realised that Christianity had to compromise with the new culture - the future was tugging too hard that way. He decided to pull off the greatest transformational operation in Western thought: assimilate Aristotle, complete with categories and methodology, into the traditional philosophy, without disturbing the eternally true blueprint of revealed religion.

It would be nice to congratulate him on succeeding. And if I could believe you when you assert that the Aristotle plus Thomas formulae are universally and eternally true (a casual indifference to history led you to state that if Christianity had sprung up in China it would have gathered the same metaphysical accretions[2]), I would not withhold my praise. But theoretical impossibilities are practical impossibilities too. Aristotle can't be rammed into Christianity. A self-sufficient, miracle-free world refuses the dictates of a supernatural God. The only things in Aristotle which really survived in the Thomist synthesis are his language and his open door on reality. But it is held open only so long as dogma is safe. At the first puff of danger it is slammed shut.

The contrast between the two strata was so glaring that Etienne Tempier, Bishop of Paris, condemned the whole enterprise in 1270 (although St. Thomas had already ruthlessly censored his own work). Tempier went further in a second condemnation in 1277.

The way to Catholic orthodoxy is paved with a thousand condemnations, but search through the files and you find none better than Tempier's as a model of shrewd diagnosis. Thomism may have saved the Church some anxious moments, but its contradictions are as obvious now as they ever were. Mixing factual analysis with assumptions about the supernatural is a risky business, as Tempier saw. When someone starts taking in reality, who will get them to stop?

A psychologist would call Thomist philosophy the workbook of a conflict staved off by repression. When a lit fuse of reasoning is about to blow some emotional mascot to smithereens, an inner censor whips out his shears. The same hatchet falls on heterodox facts. As always, though, the repressed material fights back, and the symptoms are seen - in this case a verbal tap dance on a heaving pavement of unease.

Scholasticism became a flood of verbiage. No group of people ever talked so much. The thicker the foliage of words, the better the protection. The patient is anxious not to see something and builds up a verbal screen to hide it. The talk is interminable and the screen turns into a space capsule. At the first opportunity it takes off, leaving the real world behind.

The Scholastic way of thinking is embarrassing. It is too clearly the product of obsession. The main procedure is to insert a pack of words between two ideas which must be held apart. This is the Scholastics' fail-safe system. Any ideological clash, they discovered, can be avoided by putting a series of verbal buffers between the two explosive terms. Of all their dialectical cartwheels, the Scholastics' favourite is Distinguo (I distinguish between...) carried to the nth degree of giddiness.

And that's the sad story of how a philosophy which emerged from the need to make contact with the world degenerated into a dervish dance to obliterate it from the mind. It also explains why it is called 'the perennial philosophy'. It has minted a context of verbal formulae

in a void of pure sound, without reference to anything
specific. Scholastics sit inside it happily, like hypo-
chondriacs in an antiseptic glass booth. There is a
permanent guarantee against infection, and, besides,
they get the impression that they dominate the world.
By brandishing three or four fine-sounding phrases they
believe they can telescope the world and adjust the
lenses till they feel they have it within their grasp. In
reality, they have regressed to the world of magic,
where thought acquires the megalomania of thinking
itself all-powerful.

Scholastic formulae have all the classic features of
a neurotic symptom. They are senseless, have the
puppet movements of externally controlled behaviour and
trail each other in a rain of repetition. I will examine
a randomly chosen example from your De Gratia ('On
Grace').

You are explaining how a believer in a state of grace
can take part in the divina natura (divine nature), and
how finite participation in an infinite reality is possible
- two sham problems which have sprung like toadstools
from a sloppy use of words. Here's your answer:

> Theology explains this possibility by pointing out
> that in the beatific vision the divine essence unites
> itself immediately with the intelligence as an almost
> formal cause of its act of knowing; it takes over the
> functions of the innate form and forces the intelli-
> gence into an immediate vision of itself. A divine
> act is therefore possible if, besides having as one
> term the divine being as it is in itself, it also has,
> from the very beginning (in the analytical faculty),
> not only the finite faculty but this faculty made real
> by the infinite essence as a quasi-form[3] .

The psychic mazes Freud discovered in the 'rat man'
pale to insignificance beside this passage. I have said
these formulae mean nothing, but failed to add 'by the
standards of philosophically sound language'. They do
have a meaning - would not be neurotic symptoms if they

did not.  But it is not the meaning which the words seem
to be explaining.  To understand it you need an analyst's
skill in cracking the code.

The neurotic symptoms (as always) push the forbidden
impulse down on one hand, but give it mental gratification
by toying with it on the other.  This unstable equilibrium
tends to slide further and further towards the second pole
as the neurosis deepens.  Even so, the gratification is
warped and flayed by censorship, and the patient's
state gets steadily worse.

This two-sided obsessive syndrome explains why
some phrases found in theology and philosophy have very
little to do with either, and clearly reflect things of a
quite different origin.

By now it should be clear why you find my method
repulsive.  You say it is 'certainly corrosive to faith'
and you may be right if by 'faith' you mean a hypnotic
state more in need of (to quote you) 'the pious emotion
of credulity' (pius credulitatis affectus) than intelligence [4]
It remains to be seen whether this hothouse orchid,
raised artificially on a soil of verbal swindling and
doctored history, in a sleep of reason, is worth anything.

I hold a different kind of faith, which doesn't close
its eyes to logic.  Blinding the intelligence is a blasphemy
against God.

## Footnotes

1.  Dickens made Mr. Gradgrind in Hard Times a human
    crocodile with teeth of fact, so teaching his readers
    to hate facts as soulless and tyrannical.  He did not,
    perhaps, fully realise that every moral truth is a
    concentration and synthesis of morally-relevant fact,
    which, if well expressed, explodes like a depth-
    charge.  (Translator)
2.  Scritti teologici, p. 204
3.  De Gratia, p. 115
4.  Scritti teologici, p. 156

'Quite candidly I must say I do not know how an intelligent young man who read your book carefully and understood it and the logic behind it could keep his Catholic faith, or at least, how he could avoid finding himself in serious difficulties - difficulties against which you offer no effective help. '

I'm afraid you have made a gaffe without precedent in the history of Catholic apologetics.  Listen a bit.

Professional clergymen have always stopped their ears against the rigour of lay thought, ever since Paul unbuckled his invective in Corinthians I: 'Where are your eggheads?  Where are your intellectuals?  Where are your smart alecks with the gift of the gab?  Hasn't God shown up the idiocy of worldly knowledge?'  Not even Luther could hold back when he had the chance to hit out at philosophy.

This is not to say Paul and Luther were blatherers out of their right minds.  Or that, like many others, they were propagandists for the irrational to hide a personal lack of logic in themselves.

Fury against logic derives from one of two diametrically opposite motives.  The common run of logic haters stand this side of logic, urging it to keep its distance. The rare ones run full tilt into it in an attempt to break through to the opposite side.  The utterances of the first group are whinings, those of the second the ravings of unhinged genius.  The unintentional acrobatics of a coward slipping up on ice are quite different from the movements of a reckless acrobat trying to achieve the impossible.

Paul and Luther belong to the second class. Paul was a virtuoso when it came to the skills of a rabbi. Luther, when he felt like it, a masterly wielder of logic. But both champed hungrily at the bit. First-rate dialectics are immediately evident when you recognise a tone of desperate dissatisfaction at the limitations of logic. The real target of this intolerance is not logic at all, but the bullying army of swollen-headed goons who take logic to be a magic carpet which will carry them anywhere. Paul and Luther hammer at people too full of themselves to feel a shiver at the murky depths of reality behind the last façade, behind objects, relationships and feelings.

Great care, therefore, is needed in keeping the two anthropological species mentally distinct. They may sometimes use the same vocabulary and may even clutch at the same symbols, but the parallel ends there. The first use the so-called contemplative life as a philosophical dug-out. Their bleatings are too pathetic to be called thought. The second reject logic as being too watery. Sprawling between them you find the believer in formal logic, bellowing out syllogisms as if he had laid hands on the world's secrets.

All three types appear in religious anthropology. The first and largest group never learn to handle concepts, and make do with symbols. Some are ingenious enough to exploit this weakness, using it to give extra flexibility to their hierarchy-scaling activities.

The third, formalistic group waste time over 'rational' proofs of the supernatural - this includes everyone from St. Anselm to the most insignificant Scholastics. They, like you, believe that 'metaphysical concepts and principles which derive directly from the idea of being' open the way to 'divine thought, which is certainly rational thought' '.

That leaves the second type, the restless acrobats. Luther's 'theology of the cross' is an excellent example of this straining after the impossible.

You've probably never noticed, Monsignor, but very

often the most intensely religious temperaments occupy
the same bodies as first-class minds. Many believers
never get beyond white witchcraft or the classic anthologies
of myths, so betraying their weak reasoning power and
weaker nerves. Only a few ever achieve refined religious
intuition. It needed Occam, a great juggler with words,
to pull out to their full, alarming proportions the implications folded up in the idea of the absolute power of
God. In so doing he overwhelmed the petty manias of
those theologians convinced they keep God in their
pocket.

After these preliminaries, I can analyse this section of
your letter in detail. The sentence is hypothetical ('any
intelligent young man who read...') and its conclusion
depends on two conditions (he must be intelligent; and
must have read my book carefully and understood it and
the logic behind it). Your preamble ('Quite candidly I
must say I do not know') is there to convey the grave
timbre of a voice primed to knock some choice remark
home in a dull audience's ears.

Your first condition is that my book must be read
by 'an intelligent young man'. If meant seriously, this
must imply that no element is lacking in his mental
equipment, not even the dissatisfaction to urge it forward.
True intelligence is a rare gift. It should not be con-
fused with the skills of a computer. Sleepwalkers can
sometimes work out sums with astonishing bravura. To
use Whitehead's image, intelligence is no more like a
calculation than cavalry charges are like barrack-square
drill.

An intelligent young man knows how to calculate
correctly, but knows what he is at, and does not overrate
his powers, unlike the rationalist who expects logic to
do the work for him and falls victim to recurrect bouts
of narcissism. An intelligent young man isn't spellbound
when word-drunk metaphysicians postulate that logic is
a compendium of innate knowledge about the Laws of
Being. He soon discovers that the axioms of logic are
as banally true as the fact that a knight in chess must

move in two directions in each move, the first at right
angles to the second, 2 squares + 1, or 1 + 2, and
never diagonally. A convention. Given the rules, the
rest is mechanical.

The conclusions wait to be yanked out of the premises.
The real foundation stone of logic is the fact that all
human brains work on the same principle. In dreams,
not even the principle of contradiction holds. Who knows
how we would reason if we had a bull's nervous system
grafted into us?

You are imagining a reader who falls into none of
these traps. He yields his trust with miserly reluctance,
broods over facts and weighs his words.

Your second condition is that he must have read Gli
osservanti carefully and have mastered it, getting inside
'the logic behind it'. Your words 'and understood it' after
'an intelligent young man who read...' are superfluous.
This reader could not help understanding it. Gli
osservanti does not unfold a bizarre charade. It reasons
over a chess board of facts.

Here too your wording is very precise. By positing
a reader who concentrates hard and won't miss a trick
in the game of logic, you exclude two possibilities: that
he might swallow the bait of some hidden emotional urge,
or that he could be fobbed off with attractive slogans
which deadened his thinking.

What, then, is the outcome? The answer is breath-
taking: 'I do not know how he could keep his Catholic
faith, or at least, how he could avoid finding himself in
serious difficulties - difficulties against which you offer
no effective help'. This is worth pondering at length.

Your reader, who is exposed to the reasoning in my
books, is not imagined a prey to some psychological
trauma, and so simply in danger of losing his faith. His
faith will either be eaten away by logic till nothing is left
- 'I do not know how he could keep his Catholic faith',
or, on the best possible hypothesis, he will find himself
in 'serious difficulties', with no available remedy [3].
These, you say, are the results which ineluctably follow
from the workings of an intelligent mind.

It is worth pointing out two of the consequences of this débâcle. The first is the fate of Scholasticism. You of the hierarchy consider it a hold-all of eternal truths, but if its effects are obliterated by a single reading of a book by a mere jurist, it must be a heap of junk. The arguments used by St. Anselm to prove God exists and that his Son 'had to' become flesh leave a smile settling on the face of your reader. But my book, if you are right, forces him to abandon his faith, flying in the face of strong sentimental ties, childhood memories, the teaching of his parents, the 'pneumatic' protective zone of grace, the indwelling of the very Holy Trinity, the protection of the Madonna, the intercessions of the Dead, the authority of theology, St. Anselm, St. Thomas, Suàrez, and the decrees of the Council of Trent, plus the marvels lately achieved by neo-Scholasticism.

There's little quibbling to be done here. You have implied all this. A shrewd student risks nothing from contact with one of your spokesmen, except getting a bit bored. Besides, he gets an excellent opportunity to do some irreverent fieldwork in linguistics, psychology, anthropology and sociology. But when your students come to me they undergo the kind of metamorphosis recounted in mystical books. When they've finished listening and reading, they aren't the same people as before. After all, you're the one who's told me that, and I can't say you're entirely wrong. But the treatment I give them isn't based on the use of dope words. Nor do I promise them a career in a million in this world, or eternal life in the next. There's no trace of a spell - only facts, and the play of logic in a light which pierces the verbal wrappings and makes cheating impossible.

The second implication of your verdict is lethal to the core of what you incorrectly call 'religious interests'. Faith is the courage to extend our intentions to the future, to build decisions on what does not yet exist. It has nothing to gain or lose from the work of the intellect. Religion is impregnable as long as it consists of a feeling or, in extreme cases, of a burning consciousness of a reality beyond the here-and-now of visible objects,

and not of judgments easily exposed as false,
'assumptions' which turn out to be the last brick on a
pyramid of other assumptions, verbal festooning, fairy
tales, or images whose genesis is easy to reconstruct
psychologically.

Logical analysis cannot lay a finger on true faith.
If 'Catholic faith' is so easily demolished by my book,
there can be no common ground between them.

Your anxiety about what will happen to the extrava-
ganzas of Catholic faith is well-founded. The serpent-
man-woman triangle in Eden, the resurrection of Christ's
body, the taking of Mary into Heaven, the miraculous
change in communion bread and wine, the incredible
flight of Loreto, and the promise made to St. Margaret
Marie Alacoque - all these crash from their pedestals.

You can't expect me to pay homage to a dogma. I
talk freely about transubstantiation, which stands or falls
by the Thomist idea of 'substance'. Hume's arguments
reduce both concept and dogma to a pulp. Don't, whatever you do, say 'Philosophical debates are of no interest
to me. Nor are theories from modern physics.
Miracles are a part of mysticism.'

A theory like St. Thomas's should never have been
made dogma, or else it should have been disowned when
found false. After describing the 'miracle' in realistic
terms, with the maximum amount of detail obtainable
with thirteenth-century vocabulary, it would be mad or
underhand to keep it on in the traditional repertoire as
a mysterious 'something-I-know-not-what', catapulting
the realistic framework over your shoulder (at least, if
you want to talk to people with twentieth-century men-
talities, rather than to thirteenth-century ghosts).

Anyway, even if you do that, St. Thomas's 'substance'
loses its status as a scientific hypothesis (it turned out
to be false, but the hypothesis was there - that there is
an inner 'core' or 'substratum' to things responsible for
their properties) and degenerates into primitive thought.

You are forced into the humiliating position of saying,
'Yes. Talk about "substance" and "accidents" is nonsense. We know perfectly well that matter is an

arrangement of energy, and that when bread and wine are blessed by a priest nothing happens. Even so, I believe they are really transformed into the body and blood of Christ. ' Why not drop the make-believe, and admit, 'It was all an invention'? What would be lost? Discarding animistic superstitions would raise the level of faith and put some backbone into religion - if religion is supposed to have some spiritual content.

A lawyer would accept the admissions made in this part of your letter as a properly drawn-up confession. After this, the only logical thing to do would be to shut up shop. What I don't understand is what induced you to make them. It is an unparalleled example of the spontaneous eruption of repressed material, not disfigured into a hysterical symptom or a convulsive gesture or leftover tremblings from a dream or a nervous tic, but a well-rounded phrase formulated with dispassionate calm. The one who gives a start is the reader, who hardly believes his own eyes. When I first looked at it I had to read it through again twice, to make sure I was seeing straight.

Footnotes

1. Corinthians 1, 20.
2. Scritti teologici, p. 26
3. Cordero, it is implied, should have been the one to come to the rescue. Quite a compliment to a suspect meddler in theology! Unfortunately he, like Colombo's reader, is driven remorselessly forward to his conclusions by a logical sequence of arguments in irreproachable style. Cordero's vice is that of arguing logically - if a is true, then so is b, and if b is true, then so is c, and so on to the very end. Colombo was right on one score, though - the power of logical reasoning never relaxes its grip on an honest mind. (Translator)

'It certainly seems to me he would find no help in making that comparison between Christian doctrine and lay culture which the bishops, in their communiqué last year, laid down as one of the characteristics of a Catholic university.'

Your letter now follows a trail of impeccable logic. If the metal of 'Catholic faith' suffers fatigue and shatters at high intellectual temperatures (true enough), the engines of your subjects' minds must be kept only just revving over. Only one other problem is left - setting the controls for selection, first and most importantly in education. Even non-Catholics realise what store you set by that. Everything else is trafficked in at market price, and no one turns a hair. But control over the minds of the young is a priceless asset, never to be surrendered. Lose that and you would lose power for ever.

    The Church is strong financially, diplomatically and politically. It may occasionally come up against a more ruthless financier, a subtler diplomat or a shrewder politician, and suffer a temporary setback. But in one thing its monopoly is absolute - the supernatural. And with it, the right to award salvation in another world. In your time you've put them all out of business: Demeter, Dionysus, Orpheus, Athis, Mithra and Iris. Now it's all yours¹.

    If you were ever deprived of that, the loss of prestige would be irreparable. The Church would have to struggle for survival, like the Orders founded for the crusades, which have degenerated into financial trusts or holding companies.

Unthinkable. If you want salvation, there's only one door to knock at: 'Extra ecclesiam nulla salus' . Throw yourself into her arms - baptism, christening, periodic spring-cleaning of the soul at confession, nourishment for it at the communion rail, and extreme unction when your time is up. The Church is a perfectly calculated golden mean, combining the advantages of a vocation for the easy skies of Heaven with firm control over this world in the meantime. Life here can be remarkably pleasant if slyness is your forte.

But sins seem to snowball catastrophically. Is there no danger that their accumulated mass may outweigh the sum total of good? What disastrous consequences for God's people may there be? Dismiss the thought. The specialists in building stockpiles of good are hard at it now: Trappists, nuns in retreat, missionaries and those wretches who volunteer for a life of hardships 'in accordance with the wishes of the Church'. But I was forgetting that limitless store of treasure - Christ's virtues, an atomic pile which produces far more good-ness for each applicant than all its contributors together ever put in. Providence has decreed that the Pope and his hierarchy will administer this inexhaustible fount. There's enough for everyone, and to spare.

Salvation is there at arm's length. What does Holy Mother ask in return? Laughably little, almost nothing. A few rites and rituals and boundless trust. Forget about that clique of madmen who want to do the trip by them-selves. Trust in Her. Leave thinking to Her. She's thought it all out once and for all. A unique laboratory of thought. Everything thinkable is there, enclosed in verbal capsules. No need to understand them. Voice them and repeat them.

When you feel doubt, club your pride and remember where the experience lies. Cranks deserve everything they get. You will choose the winning side. If you have the misfortune to meet poisonous critics, don't stop to argue. Sneer contemptuously and walk straight ahead. All empty chatter. You have twenty centuries of accrued wisdom on your side - cast-iron brain, from St. Basil to Jean Guitton. If anyone has any doubts left after that, they should open St. Thomas's Summa Theologiae. Enough to leave them gasping. 613 questions dissected in thousands of articles, each giving arguments for and against, and proving the right conclusion. He even listed possible objections, with the correct replies. A healthy brain need look no further.

To keep the faithful in their rut of psychological subjection, ritual is not enough. A 'scientific' apparatus is needed. When St. Thomas was alive, the Church wasn't pushed. It seemed to have all known science stored within it, even if those damned Averroists[3] at the Faculty of Arts in Paris University were kicking up a fuss.

As late as 1850, a reasonable showing could still be made. The disastrous collapse of the Ptolemaic system had been superseded with remarkable aplomb. The 'philosophical' foundations of Catholicism still looked as if they could prop something up, despite heckling from Hegel. Then one tidal wave after another crashed over the monolith - Marx, Darwin and Freud, and the great names in modern physics.

Now here are the bishops with their communiqué quoted by you, laying it down that a Catholic university should 'compare Christian doctrine and lay culture'. So lay culture exists. The outsiders have achieved official recognition.

But it was hardly wise to talk about a 'comparison between Christian doctrine and lay culture'. 'Comparison' means placing two things side by side to get a deeper understanding of each - similarities, differences and analogies. Exactly what Gli osservanti does! I feel sure it caused a frenzy in the minds of many Catholics precisely because it made this particular comparison, in breadth and depth.

What do you mean by 'comparison', then? You certainly don't mean a truce should be made in the warfare between the two. The hot-headed apologists of the second century tried that and concluded that Plato was worth at least as much as the first five books of the Bible. Teilhard de Chardin, their modern successor, wanted to arrange an honourable peace between Catholicism and science, after drubbing his own views into the latter. But you are deeply hostile to him. Not, of course, because he was a muddled thinker, but because his efforts were judged an impertinent encroachment onto ground held sacred to theology.

No peace is possible between the two worlds. No Teilhard can arrange one. Catholicism hurls up clusters of myths, assumptions disproved by everyday experience, verbal formulae worshipped like antiques from privileged ages and now repeated meaninglessly, and remarks of the 'God from God, light from light' variety, which insult intelligence. Science gives you a wealth of facts rooted out by hard work, reasoning which stands its ground, and respect for words.

The idea of a supremely autonomous soul-substance shattered into a thousand pieces as soon as it was discovered that the life of the psyche is as rigidly determined by causal factors as the sway of the tides and the growth of a plant. And the so-called 'first principles of reasoning' took a beating they can never recover from when it became known that each social group creates its own. The creation of Adam and Eve, the sins of apple-eating in the garden of Eden, and the father-to-son handing down of original sin with each act of reproduction cannot be asserted with a straight face by anyone minimally acquainted with evolutionary biology.

I would like to dwell for a moment on this point. You yourself admit[4] that the Catholic authorities initially condemned evolutionary theory, forcing the faithful to believe that Genesis was literal truth. Seventy years after the theory's appearance, your position was too dangerous, and you took to your heels, leaving Genesis to fend for itself. Pius XII blandly informed the usual mastiffs of orthodoxy, clamouring for another turn of the screw, that one Galileo in the history of the Church was enough. You follow suit, 'As the teaching of the Magisterium stands at present...

this question is theologically free'[5] .

After evolution had been let out of the pillory, one
of its consequences had to be faced. If the human species
has appeared through evolution (even country priests
know this now), its origins lie not in one individual (from
whose body a rib was extracted by God to make one
woman) but in various individuals - those whose genetic
characteristics fell, for the first time in their lineage,
within those we define as human. In other words, we
come from a variety of genetic stocks.

This flatly contradicts the dogma of Original Sin.
The Holy Spirit, speaking through the mouths of the
Council of Trent, talked about the sin of Adam, 'single
in origin and handed on with every act of reproduction'.
When it comes to dogma, interpreters are allowed no
free play. If the Council of Trent ruled that one man
handed original sin on to all others, that's the end of it.
Files closed. But in case a flicker of doubt was left in
anyone's mind, a second dogma was formulated to tell
us how to interpret the first. The first Vatican Council
(1870) said the interpretation of dogma has been fixed
'once and for all' (the meanings trail on, mummified,
through the centuries) 'by Holy Mother Church'[6] .

You deny that there can be any contradiction between
science and dogma until science 'gets to the point of
proving the multiple origin of the human race...as a
matter of certainty'[7] . And what if it did? You sin-
cerely hope it doesn't. The trouble is, it has already.
Evolutionary theory would be senseless if it did not
imply it. Your only comment is that the origins of the
human race are 'wrapped in mystery'. But until fifty
years ago they were crystal clear. Genesis told us
everything we wanted to know. Only 100 years ago we
knew the date of the creation of the world to the nearest
year, from the biblical genealogies...4004 B.C.

On the origin of women the mists lift. The Bible
and the Church Fathers, you tell us, leave no doubts
and 'The present Church authorities rightly demand that
we accept their teaching in interpreting the Genesis
account as historical fact'[8] . Eve was born miraculously

from Adam's rib. God decided this 'to found and to display the twofold relationship between the sexes in the family - equality and co-operation on one hand, male supremacy on the other'.

An unbeliever will smile or shake his head in despair, but ' the position of someone who won't accept miracles freely willed by God is more irrational than that of someone who admits they may have happened, and only waits for the proof...' Which proofs in this case? Bone exhibits from Eve? But a bit later I find you admitting that 'not everything is as clear and final on this point as some people seem to suppose'[9]. The fog of confusion is there after all.

The progressive dilution of the Church's certainty over Adam is a splendid example of how theologians scatter for cover when the threat from scientific research becomes too pressing. I would like you to tell me how any scientist can work seriously in such a setting without falling into heterodoxy, and how any orthodox scientist can keep his self-respect. If 'Catholic' is given the reactionary meaning you attach to it, a Catholic university is a contradiction in terms. It must either cease to be a university - a place where culture is formed by critically-minded people - or cease to be Catholic. The two concepts are on a collision course.

What is traditional Catholicism, after all? A mammoth cloche protecting images from a dream world, false assertions about facts and illogical verbal formulae - the residue of an indefensible theory about reality which included or includes the devil's tail and angels busy over the accountancy side of indulgences.

Choose between two attitudes: scientific honesty, and the risk of making mistakes (only theologians have infallibility on tap), and theological blustering. The theory for the second was written up by Father Gemelli in the opening article in the first number of Vita e pensiero ('Life and Thought') published in December 1914. The symptomatic title was Medioevalismo ('Medievalism') This manifesto of Catholic anti-culture offers few crumbs for a hungry intellect, but is an enormous cache of psychological source material, an ideal text for my analysis of Scholastic formulae as fetishes and defence mechanisms[10].

With his usual arrogance Gemelli bragged, 'I find this poor modern culture pitiable', but soon after admitted it frightened him because 'it strangles souls'. Another kind of culture was needed, which would answer 'the deepest and most unquenchable longings of the human spirit'. All roads led to the Middle Ages, whose 'noble traditions have regrettably been broken off from the Renaissance onwards, for a variety of reasons'.

It was no use trying for a compromise. 'Our enemy', modern culture since, and including, the Renaissance 'carries with it the signs of its death'. It mustn't be offered 'truce, quarter, or the honour of arms'. True Catholics detest the rehabilitation of Galileo. Why was the Holy Office so soft on him? Why not roast him? He, Gemelli, would have had no doubts. That rogue had shamed the skies by trampling on Dante's theory of astronomy.

Gemelli, a brawling Franciscan (he manages to give the impression he's shouting, even off the printed page) goes on to tell his spiritual story. The memoirs of a man whose muddleheadedness marched alongside his uncontrollable aggressiveness. Science left him cold because it gave no answers to the 'ultimate questions'. He had dabbled in philosophy, but no luck there. He had grazed past modernism and at last found his home in Christianity, 'the only great general conception of the universe which answers the needs of the human spirit'. Men with a streak of Gemelli in them - a bully whose moods veered like a weathervane - go hunting for a mental cage to live in. He found it in Scholasticism.

At first the mealy language put him off. But after fighting off his initial distaste he found a universe of final truths. Everything thinkable had been spelt out once and for all between 1100 and 1200 - a conclusion worthy of a crass intellect.

Worried that the point had been left in some doubt,

Gemelli repeated it in a style that became fashionable a few years later and reached its climax in the ranting invective of Fascism. As a proud enemy of modern culture he had a predilection for Pius IX's Syllabus of Errors as a source of inspiration. Pius wrote it to condemn those who said 'the Roman Pontiff can and must reconcile himself to, and compromise with, progress, liberalism and modern culture'.

Gemelli went on from there. Cultural philanthropy was getting out of hand - they wanted to open universities to the working classes and high schools to girls! Then there is a hilarious passage about the difficulties of living in a world where scientific progress forces people to know too much. Culture is seen as an untidy mass which grows by addition. He preferred systems as tightly closed as unripe pine-cones. The simple ideas must 'contain' the complex ones. Anyway, he can't put up with that positivist liking for 'brute facts'. A splinter of an idea is worth far more than a million facts, and the only ideas worth worrying about are those at the top of his scale of values: God, Soul, Nature of Man, etc.,

The illiterate Catholic peasant is wiser ('knows more') than an intellectual miscreant. Gemelli drew up his own definition of doctrine: you need 'a general conception of the universe' (already summarised in the Catechism); judge everything by that; refuse everything outside it; be intolerant with whoever disagrees.

Gemelli like that word, 'intolerant', and left unforgettable documents behind to prove it. Still nagged by the suspicion he hadn't put the final gloss on his opinions, he repeated he was 'deeply hostile to modern culture'. 'Try talking to cultured people nowadays about miracles and they refuse to follow your reasoning', behaviour which calls aloud for punishment. The pity is, the authorities are soft nowadays. The Middle Ages weren't so squeamish. Robert le Bougre dealt with the Albigensians in grand style, murdering an entire civilisation with extraordinary savagery. Fresh prodigies on that model - he gave no details, but the innuendo is clear - would mean pogroms of medieval thoroughness.

There were too many Jews, Freemasons, modernists, freethinkers, atheists and other slippery customers around. His recipe for them appears in a filthy article published in the August 1924 issue of Vita e pensiero:

> Felice Momigliano - Jew, secondary schoolteacher, great philosopher and great Socialist - has committed suicide. Spineless journalists have been shedding crocodile-tear obituaries over him. Some point out he had been Rector of the Mazzini University. Others that he was a positivist after the decline of positivism. But if not only positivism, but socialism freethinking, too - if not only Momigliano, but all Jews, people carrying on the work of the Jews who crucified our Lord - if they all died, wouldn't the world be a better place? The liberation would be even more complete if, before dying, they repented and asked to be baptised.

Baptised or not, he wanted them dead. Who can guess how much his fancy would have been tickled by the story of an execution for heresy celebrated at Logroño on 24 August 1719. The culprit was, funnily enough, a crypto-Jew. They were about to light the logs round the stake and the monks (one of them is telling the story) were going into fits to wring a last minute confession out of their victim. He finally yielded and told them everything they wanted to hear. His saviours were now in high glee. Even the executioner, who had been standing ready out of sight behind the pile of wood, was so moved he came up to have a look. He had called his crypto-Jew a swine, but the swine was now his brother, and he dropped to his knees to ask him forgiveness. A scene which would jerk tears out of the stoniest hearts.

The story-teller, an expert in the reckless arts of soul-saving, didn't let his feeelings run away with him, though. Conversions come and go. Strike while the iron is hot. It would be crazy to leave time for second thoughts! With a deliberately casual air, he wandered round to the back of the pyre and whispered to the executioner that there wasn't a moment to lose. The executioner tiptoed up behind the new convert and throttled him".

Every detail in this tableau exudes delicacy: a sense of love for one's neighbour and of work well done in the service of God. Just think, too, they were able to let themselves go like that in the year 1719, after Voltaire had been born (and with him the Age of Monsters). Those defilers of the Holy - the personnel of the Enlightenment, with that sordid invention of theirs, the Revolution, burned their bridges with that civilised age where you breathed the transcendent deep into your lungs. The last word hasn't been said yet, though. Spiritual values are indestructible.

But to get back to Gemelli. His synopsis of 'Culture' presupposes a 'general conception of the universe':

> God three in one: Man who hears Satan speaking; the fall of Adam; the coming of Christ, Saviour of mankind, his passion and death as a means of persuading people to join the Church; the Church as a supernatural medium for telling mankind the truth it needs and for guiding it towards its goals; the Pope, supreme and infallible Master; the Judgment, the rewarding of the good and the punishing of the wicked; and, to end this marvellous epic, blessed souls who take their rest in eternal glory, praising their Creator.

Get back to the Middle Ages we must, Gemelli says, and most of all in philosophy 'because being a philosopher means solving the basic problems of life and, besides a Christian...is a philosopher par excellence'. I suspect Gemelli was using 'philosopher' here as you use it when saying[12] a doctor can't explain 'a disease in terms of a metaphysical principle or by reference to permission from divine providence' because 'he would stop being a scientist and become a philosopher'. In both cases 'philosopher' means 'dabbler in loose talk whose meaning can never be pinned down'.

82

Gemelli's manifesto has a flag-waving finale. He appeals to 'anyone who has an Italian soul' to collaborate with him, the expert in restoring the Middle Ages, 'so that Italy, in rediscovering a tradition which is all ours, will rediscover the means and the strength to make it live again'.

Thirty-six years later Gemelli was still slinging out verdicts. 'Catholics can't hold psychoanalytical views, or accept them, or agree to be analysed, or let a sick husband or wife be analysed' because 'psychoanalysis [is] a danger, the unhealthy fruit of Freud's gross materialism'[13]. Even so, Gemelli's wild stomping fits perfectly into the psychoanalytical picture - a refusal to accept reality, an aggressive reaction to anything which recalls the repressed material, regression appearing here as escape into the Middle Ages, and hermetic retreat into the artificial world of Scholastic mock-logical formulae. Thirty-six years of this regime had their ruinous effect, as anyone can check today by going to the Catholic University of Milan.

Repression on this scale is a public disaster. The individual pays the price of a frenzied waste of energy in internal censorship, society the price of blockheaded tyranny. Gemelli, Fascist to the core[14] and a Jew-hater, left behind him memorable evidence of his intolerance, factiousness, bad taste and despotism.

Supreme master of the Catholic University for over thirty-five years, Gemelli imposed or tolerated execrable methods of government - everything from a spying system to the head-hunting régime of the congregations[15], from terrorism to the calculations of a party manager. These are the account books of an uninterrupted flow of power based on the motto 'Back to Medievalism!' If Catholic anti-culture has ever produced anything fit to be shown in public, in daylight, it's time it was brought out now.

Footnotes

1. Absorption of the Protestant Churches is going forward steadily. An ironic working of the dictum, 'To

him that hath shall be given; but from him that hath
not shall be taken away even that which he hath'.
The merchandise here is spiritual totalitarianism.
In religion there are no monopoly laws.  (Translator)
2.  'No salvation outside the Church'.
3.  Followers of Averroes, the great Arab philosopher
who gave the scientific attitude a decisive push forward.
4.  Scritti teologici, p. 656f.
5.  Ibid., p. 659
6.  'Sacrorum dogmatum in sensus perpetuo est retinendus,
quem semel declaravit sancta Mater Ecclesia'.
7.  Ibid., p. 674
8.  Ibid., p. 678
9.  Ibid., p. 677
10. See Chapter VII, pp. 68-72
11. F. Fita, 'La Inquisicion de Logrono y un judaizante
quemado en 1719', Boletin de la Real Academia de
la Historia, 1904, p. 457 f., quoted by H. Kamen,
L'Inquisizione spagnola, translated by R. Petrillo,
Milan, 1966, p. 213.
12. Scritti teologici, p. 663
13. 'Psicoanalisi e cattolicesimo', Vita e pensiero, 1950,
p. 254
14. No shortage of examples.  One range-finding insult
lumps together 'slant-eyed international freemasonry,
Communist demagogy, the insolence of people
wallowing in wealth, and Protestant phariseeism'
(see Vita e pensiero, November 1935).  Italy is
tightly bunched round the King and Mussolini against
these forces 'as if it was a single mind and a single
heart'.  It has responded with 'such hardworking and
untroubled calmness of mind and with such a unani-
mously virile attitude as to prove to what political
heights Italy has been raised by a few years of
Fascism'.

You, too, Monsignor had your say in an article entitled
'Guerra coloniale e teologia morale' ('Colonial War and
Moral Theology').  I have been unable to obtain a copy of
this, but imagine it is a theological apologia for the

campaign against Abyssinia. I have seen 'Guerra e pace nel pensiero cristiano' ('War and Peace in Christian Thought') in Rivista di filosofia neoscolastica, July 1940, where your style oscillates between that of a colonel and that of a casuist.

The problem of conscientious objection is smartly set aside. Citizens must fight for their country because wars are just, but whether a war is just or not has to be decided by the authorities. No citizen can escape his duty to kill and be killed just because he disagrees with them, unless he is 'perfectly and absolutely sure' a war is unjust. But this is a theoretical possibility, never a real one. Over and above what you call the obvious motives for fighting (which might appear insufficient to a sceptic) there are, in all probability, other, hidden ones known only to the competent authorities, and these would be enough to override and completely reverse his private judgment. (The authorities couldn't reveal their hidden motives, because it would be against the public good.)

If the thoughts of the French had always followed this bent, France would still be a Merovingian monarchy, assuming, of course, that Clovis's bloody rise to, and seizing of power is accepted as legitimate. But here the conversion of the Franks was at stake, so he had the full backing of the Pope, two considerations which render all others insignificant.

'I am sure you will realise that, in writing the above, I have had a heavy heart. I have written after meditation and I have been thinking, above all, of the good of the young, as is my duty.'

This is the crux of the matter. The rest is sparring. 'The good of the young' is an ambiguous phrase. It depends on the model flashing in your mind. You are thinking about a crafty young man, immune to moral passion, yearning for protectors, on the look-out for good opportunities and determined not to let them slip, thick-skinned as to the opinions of others when he does something mean, ready to trample over competitors, capable of brooding over long-standing grudges hidden under a sly smile, obedient to the point of delirium, obliging, a clever small talker, a silky smile on his lips and a viper's tongue behind them, devoid of intellectual curiosity, too intent on his career to think about anything else, a man who doesn't recognise that women exist - or even books! except, of course, the ones he has to quote from.

    I don't hesitate to admit that the Catholic University, as it was and partly is, but may soon no longer be, offers this human species a unique opportunity: a good chance to get inside the Christian Democrat ruling class (examples of well-upholstered success spring to mind). In his favour he will have selection techniques openly aimed at excluding intelligence, the backing of church and lay patrons, and that only vaguely defined homosexual air that can be breathed in communities run by priests.

There you have the ideal training for a good life.

But what about the other young men...the young men with backbone, the clear thinkers who look you straight in the eye, eager to learn, the religious spirits, the ones who are thirsting for justice, the ones who say what they mean and can't stand mutterings and whisperings, the ones who set themselves and others high standards, the moral vertebrates who are nauseated by the typical Catholic success-figure, the ones who can't stand compromise. Are you, Monsignor, thinking about their good, or are you pretending they don't exist? They do exist and are far more restless than your informers tell you. The problem must, I contend, be discussed with reference to them.

For this anthropological group, a Catholic education, as you interpret it, is the mass-production of unhappiness. Firstly consider the intellectual side. These boys are intelligent and lose no time in realising how little the big doses of belief handed out like miracle pills are worth. They have a very rich emotional life, unlike the career-men (cold-blooded creatures ready to dance a bear-dance in the market place if that will earn them an advantage). The mock-truths have been hammered into them like nails. But they stand in ever-greater danger of wearing themselves out in unsuccessful attempts at evasion, as, with the passing of time, they become emotionally attached to what their intelligence despises. If lucky, they just manage to fight clear of these inner conflicts, which then become a matrix for introspective subtlety.

But another outcome is far more common. They drag themselves along in two parallel lives, never able to win free, but never able to throttle the impulse to know and understand, never able to commit intellectual suicide. And if, worst of all, they commit this intellectual suicide, they live like larvae, rolling away from every shaft of light: it would kill them if they looked at it, because their personality is built entirely of a rind of self-protection.

Being strong enough to accept all kinds of truth saves a lot of psychic suffering. This should be the aim of education. In Freudian terms, progress consists in annexing to the ego, which is responsible for reasoning, all the territory which can be wrenched away from the id, which is the sewer of sensual drives, and from the super-ego, which is the slave-driver inside us, two masters who are equally loathsome and far more alike than is commonly thought. This process does nothing to damage the richness of the instinctive life, including the life of the imagination, and subtracts nothing from the rigour of moral judgment. Reaching a good balance quickly between these three factors means, simply, being free, if by 'free' you mean 'fully conscious of what you do when you make decisions.'

The Scholastics' model of the universe is so beautiful it makes you feel like fainting: the earth stands at the centre of the universe; from the moon up there is a perfect, incorruptible celestial sphere; our souls are immortal and heaven and hell fight to win them; our souls were lost, but the Son of God came to save them; who can imagine their full worth if He died to save them; after death we will see God and a metaphysical universe full of constellations of essences; logic and mathematics are portholes on to these eternal constellations.

You have to be an aesthetic boor not to feel the beauty of this vision. But it's one thing to be bowled over by a pretty picture, another to lose your head. A trance is not a philosophy. Don't forget, either, that aesthetic emotions can be felt in response to reality. The image of a necessary pattern in things fills the tiniest events with immense meaning.

A Catholic education is as great a disaster morally as it is intellectually. I don't want to tone down my remarks. Hatred for your neighbour, lurid malice, vulgar exhibitionism, impudence, whining, hypocrisy and cynicism all grow better in the shade thrown by the Catholic tree of power than elsewhere. What shakes you with the force of a nightmare is that no one moves a finger to root up these evils, as if this filth was necessary to the flowering of grace.

The young man I am imagining has learnt the moral

strictness of Judaism, the foundation of Christianity.
But when he looks round him, in a place where Catholic
militancy flourishes, he seems to be living through a
bad dream - he has got lost in a canvas by Hieronymus
Bosch, perhaps the one about the good thief, the Road to
Calvary. Those faces send a shiver through him. He
doesn't dare say so, because he doesn't trust his own
judgment. But he's understood perfectly, the truth's
soon driven home. If he opens his mouth, and he's
lucky, they'll laugh in his face, 'What, are you living in
the clouds?'. Those men of the world are surprised by
nothing. A person who's worthless knows it, and smiles.
The only mock-moral jerk of emotion which ever runs
through him is the fury of a stone-thrower venting his
spleen on a victim, left a free hand by religious motives,
his eyes starting out of his head, face contorted by anger,
hands and body shaking convulsively, the doer of a holy
work of justice. In the intervals between these canni-
balesque parties, he goes off to church, prays at the
top of his voice, swallows wafers and lapses into ecstasy.

'It's not our fault' the defender of the system protests,
'You find men like that everywhere. As soon as we can,
we'll put him out of harm's way. Don't take individuals
- or, worse, the dregs - for the institution.'
    This is stacking the cards. Only a fool would attack
the Church he is born into because it contains some
obscene figure. The question is whether there is any
connection between the properties of the system and the
calibre of the men in it. Individuals make up the system.
But it is the system, through its norms, which moulds
them. The individuals come and go, the institution
remains.
    The conclusion appears inevitable. If not the average
creature of the system, at least the man who has all the
requisites for success in its hierarchy, he is the man
who has been accepted by the system and moulded to its
shape. The inferences are not comforting for Holy
Mother Church. It is she who wants children of this
kind, she who gives birth to them, suckles them and

89

protects them with her love (the image is Calvin's).
They are useful to her in all the manoeuvres which
involve her innumerable earthly interests.

As soon as Luther, a monk burning with faith and
moral conviction, encountered this sociological constant,
he identified it as Antichrist. Anyway, leaving aside
mythology of this kind, the fraternities of power, with
their deliberate manipulation of the individual, appear
in a more and more diabolical light the closer you look.

The apologist has his answer, 'This is the degene-
ration of a system which inevitably has to rely on human
nature, with its weaknesses. Mankind drags along with
it original sin. Many fail to live up to their ideals. But
the system must be judged by its teachings, independently
of what it does. Besides, religious typology doesn't end
with the moral thug. He may be the most conspicuous
but don't be biased. There are others, and better ones
- the mystic, and the high idealist who sacrifices all to
obedience. '

This argument is of great importance, and merits
careful discussion. There are two kinds of mysticism
- the finer one, distilled from the intellectual rare-
faction of 'negative theology' (God is in secret, beyond
our power to imagine) and the other, grosser variety,
which could be called 'religious sensuality'.

The first is a sure sign of a temperament out of the
common run. But when it buds in a Catholic setting,
the system hurries to repress it, for its own perfectly
valid reasons. Meister Eckhardt is treated as an out-
law. The second type, the predominant one in a
Catholic setting, wallows in instinct. Father Gemelli,
who studied psychology and psychiatry, should have
been able to diagnose the erotomania of St. Marguerite
Marie Alacoque, the founder of the cult of the Sacred
Heart. These remarks should not stir controversy. I
make them not out of contempt for this kind of ecstasy,
but to place them in the correct perspective - the sexual
one. There's nothing reprehensible about that. All or
nearly all beauty in the world springs from sex, through
a phantasmagoric play of inhibitions, sublimations and

projections. And eunuchs are unfortunate, on the spiritual plane too, even if they're to your taste. But it is the moral side which concerns us here, not the aesthetic. Judged as moral experience, the orgasms of Marguerite Marie or St. Teresa are exactly equivalent to the feats of 'O' in The Story of O. There is no difference on the male side either. When the mystic bridegroom penetrates his trembling victim he is being no more moral than René, Pierre or Sir Stephen.

Besides, religious sensuality in men contains its own backlash. It appears as a pause between fits of aggression. Once these men emerge from their ecstatic swooning they are formidable persecutors.

Abelard was unlucky enough to encounter two of them. First he was condemned by the Council of Soissons in 1121 to throwing one of his books on the fire and to living in retreat in the Monastery of Saint-Médard.

Eighteen years later William of Saint-Thierry, author of the oily little treatise De natura et dignitate amoris, sounded the alarm, warning St. Bernard of other suspect statements by Abelard. The Madonna's lover didn't need telling twice. Abelard was privileged to be judged at a council at Sens in 1141, in presence of Louis VII. St. Bernard, renowned heretic-hunter, refused to let him speak: does he think the bishops and abbots of the two provinces of Sens and Reimy have come to hear him arguing? 'Keep your philosopher's arguments down your throat; speak only to deny you said these things or to retract them'. The attack was so vicious that Abelard was unable to get a hearing, and withdrew, appealing to the Pope. The Council condemned Abelard's errors, leaving the final judgment on his person to the Pope.

Abelard started off for Rome, where he had friends to help him, but at Lyons caught up with the news that Innocent II had confirmed the sentence, condemning him to imprisonment in a monastery. In the meantime the Madonna's sweetheart had been working like a slave. He sent the Pope not only the accusations against Abelard, but also a letter attacking Abelard's insertion of

philosophy in theology, and ten letters to the Roman
Curia, in ascending order of violence. The formulae
used to bring pressure to bear ran like this, 'If you are
a son of the church, if you recognise your mother's
nipples, don't leave her in danger, don't deny her your
arm now, in this time of tribulation''. The heretic
Abelard was guilty of holding less unreasonable views
than the official ones. After his condemnation he ran
into Peter the Venerable, who welcomed him in a
fatherly way into the Abbey of Cluny, where he got permission to keep him. After recanting, Abelard went
back to the breast of Holy Mother and passed the last
months of his life a model prisoner, so much so that his
warder, Peter, gave him full praise for it afterwards.

Abelard's tragic end leads into the answer to the
second part of the objection. It is true that the Church
has always contained people who have put up with the
vilest mistreatment, not out of cowardice, but as a form
of heroic self-discipline. Anthropologically, this
attitude is worth far more than revolt, because it keeps
the tormented man in a state of tension which generates
vast accumulations of spirituality. Big leaps in spiritual
quality spring from ascetic renunciation. Without
pressure from the Church these prodigious events would
never happen. But the Church has little to boast about
because of this. Its part is necessarily that of a persecutor. The secondary consequences are produced
against its wishes. If it depended on Her, the inequalities
would be razed flat. Besides, beyond a certain point,
psychic energy originally built up in obedience blows
the structures of control sky high. The restrictive
models are worth too little to be tolerated.

Among Catholics there are individuals of strong
moral character, just as, but in higher proportions, they
are found among Mennonites and Baptists. What would
have to be proved is that they are moral because they
are Catholics, because of the skein of doctrines, human
examples and educational practices built into the system's
routine. The system does not produce moral men. It
has difficulty in putting up with them. It usually ejects

92

them.  Morality means love of clearness; in ecclesiastical circles the first thing you learn is the vagueness of words.  The homo moralis follows inflexible rules; the Catholic spirit, from the doctrine of the casuists to the selling of indulgences, has always carved out for itself a history of pure craftiness, aimed at severing this trait from its deservedly unpleasant consequences and moneying it with their pleasant, undeserved opposites. Acting morally means being ready to back the losing side, and knowing you're doing so, in the conviction that the voice of conscience is worth more than all the riches of the world.  To plunge headlong into this abyss you need the iron nerves of a gambler.

The archetype orthodox Catholic success-figure is an extremely crafty individual, brilliant at calculating gains and losses and with a strong inclination towards cheating.  He won't move a finger unless some inviting advantage is beckoning.  If you insisted that the Greek gods had taken over power in heaven, he would first check the information with his most reliable informants, and, if convinced, would render full and due homage to the family of Zeus.

To cut a complex story short, the young man I have been imagining finds himself no better off morally than intellectually in this habitat.  Plunged into anguish by the hostile environment around him, he searches for the root causes in himself.  When someone comes up against a solid wall of human opposition on every side, they have to have a thick layer of psychological armour not to give ground.  If this young man survives, he may, perhaps, be allowed to drag his wounded self along as best he can.  By now his hard head has been softened up beautifully.  But there will be real trouble if he ever tries to raise his head proudly again - a crazy idea.  If that happens, the punishment will burn any desire out of him to try tampering with the system.  Finally smashed by his failed attempts at rebellion, and convinced he has deserved everything, he may then make a few feeble attempts to join up with the herd.  But the door will be slammed in his face time after time.  To succeed in some things, you must be built for the job. What else can he try? Building up an inner world of ideas and imagination to make up for the filthy one he's forced to live in.

Is this 'thinking of the good of the young'?

### Footnotes

1. This phrase appears in the appeal to Guido Pisano, letter 334, see Migne, PL 182; 539

'It is also my duty to inform the Dean of the Faculty and
the Rector of the contents of this letter. But, because
of the respect I feel for you personally, I am ready to
hold a frank conversation with you when you like. I
remember you and your family in my prayers.'

The last bit of your letter gives a clear insight into the
workings of the ecclesiastical mind. A sect corresponds
to a male archetype. It is sensitive to quality, uses
rigorous logic, aims at perfection, and generates high
levels of moral tension. But the Church is a huge womb,
and is glad of it. Being its own midwife robs it of a
taste for the unique. It is interested in the species, not
the individual. Power wielded on a vast scale implies
indifference towards an atypical case, a predisposition
for a system of low moral and intellectual tensions, a
high priority on obedience and a quest for uniformity.
    When I was fifteen, the headmaster of my oratory,
in entrusting me to a colleague who had to set me
spiritual exercises, told him about my incorrect tendency
to take things seriously instead of 'smoothly'. This
adverb reveals more than was intended about your
educational models. The interior landscapes of the mind
are irrelevant. What counts is respect for authority.
Being able to count on a conditioned reflex of obedience
would be the ideal, but calculations of sheer advantage
aren't to be sneezed at either as movers of men. Clero-
cracies offer easy careers to unbelievers sly enough to
keep in step.
    You can put all your cards on the table when you're

dealing with an unbelieving believer. Always a relief.
One of the pieces of wreckage left behind by the temporal
power of the Pope is the atheist whose respect for priests
lies in the marrow of his bones. Because priests are
built into the weight-bearing structures of power.

One of these men, who nearly had a nervous breakdown at the thought of seeing this book in print, kept
prodding me with sidelong looks and innuendos worthy
of a devil's advocate. 'When on earth has an individual
got the better of the Church?' Yes, in the last analysis,
under the glitter and satisfaction of rich hangings,
precious metals, tapestries and pieties, and below the
spellbinding power of the ritual, the system is atheist.
Endless cud-chewing about the transcendent is a mask
for the religion of power, or else turns easily into a
crude philosophy of immanence (worship of God deviated
into worship of a hierarchy of power).

Its sociological needs determine the course of the
Church's policy from top to bottom. The most striking
example is false tolerance. Gribaldi Mofa, the sixteenth-
century jurist from Turin who became an independent
Protestant, was relatively free from attack at Padua,
while at Tübingen and Geneva his work was subjected to
terrible poundings. The conclusion, however, is not
that Catholics are less intolerant than Protestants, but
that they don't feel clashes of ideas. The fanatical
persecution of Mofa by the Protestants and Reformers
was a childish disease in a spiritual temperament rich
in promise: Catholic cynicism has had an uninterrupted
history. Four hundred years have passed since the
attacks on that upstanding Piedmontese jurist. For the
last 300 years religious persecution has been unknown
in Protestant countries. In Catholic countries the
desire to persecute has never lulled, even if good
opportunities are harder to come by, thanks to infuriating
situations which must be faced with clenched teeth.
Protestant theology is a landmark in culture. Catholic
theology peters on in seminaries as a mass of suffo-
cating formulae, and has no hope of being revived,
because its practitioners know only too well what

disasters would lie in store if laymen ever got their
hands on the tricks of the trade.

Let's have a good look at it from close to, this
bland Catholic nonchalance which the apologists insistently
hold up for comparison with Protestant extremism. If
this blandness is taken to mean that in Catholic countries
there are people who do things with impunity which would
never be tolerated in a society consisting of moral vertebrates, this comment is spot on. The protection of
Holy Mother opens up rich careers compatible with whole
casebooks of vices. A fair dose of immorality is not
considered harmful; on the contrary, it is a necessary
requisite for acceptance. Besides, you of the hierarchy
don't want to get mixed up in ideas and ideology. A man
who punctiliously carries out all the obeisances required of a spiritual serf can leave his mind a warren
of vice. Real tolerance, however, is not quite that, it
presupposes respect for the other person and would
therefore be out of place in a Catholic setting. Only two
classes of things are tolerated there - those too strong
to be suppressed and those which cause only marginal
irritation. An inevitable consequence of the Church's
complete indifference to the life of the mind is that the
most bizarre kinds of recklessness can find full satisfaction in private, the only price being a steady rent
of orthodox behaviour in public.

Erasmus is the prototype of the integrated unbeliever. This friend of power made his name by
kneading his malleable unbelief to whatever shape was
required.

The Catholic doctrine of power sweats black pessi-
mism from all its pores. An immortal soul and an
otherworldly destination for the faithful are easily
bartered for the misery you inflict on their humility
here on earth, educating them to it with this refrain,
'You are a bag of filth. You deserve nothing. Kill off
the animal in your head. Strike your thoughts dead.
Vegetate in my womb. '

Where its own apparatus is concerned, the Church
reacts like a beast of prey. The worst possible danger

is that someone may provide an example of spiritual
independence, and spread the disease. These cases
rile, and provoke the system, because they strike at its
foundations. It couldn't go on reproducing itself if its
subjects were woken from their complacent doze. When
repression is decided on, no finesse is spared: fire,
the killer's knife, threats of torture, life imprisonment
- these are only examples, and not the worst. The
cases bulk large in the history books: Arnaldo da Brescia,
Giordano Bruno, Paolo Sarpi, Galileo, Giannone and so
on.

You are incredibly adroit at exploiting the medicinal
properties of terror. Seven centuries ago it was enough
to issue a summons to get Occam trundling from Oxford
to Avignon. Then he wore his nerves to shreds in a long
wait while the commission of enquiry rummaged around
in the intricate heresies of his fifty-six suspect articles.

Holy Mother was strong enough to make anyone
shudder then. It mustn't be thought, though, that she
counts for little nowadays. In every sphere, from banking
to the culture industry, she has long arms at her disposal. But times have changed, and persecution has to
be transacted under the counter. Besides, the persecutors get caught up at every step in a tantalising
juridical network of restrictions, an invention of the
Enlightenment which can never be sufficiently deplored.
'When will we be able to cut free?' shout the wild men like
Father Gemelli, tugging at the leash and sweating for
the moment when they will be able to make a clean
sweep of lay culture, dating from the Tennis Court Oath
on - no! what am I saying? - from the very beginnings
of the Renaissance.

These limitations exist, and for the moment must
be respected. Thinking is no longer considered a crime.
The Italian Constitution guarantees freedom of thought,
of speech and of teaching methods. It is not a crime if
you are not a Thomist, if you prefer Rudolf Carnap to
Etienne Gilson and Hans Kelsen to Father Taparelli, or
if you think that moral rules are a product of society
rather than offshoots of a divine revelation, or if you

dare to point out that phallic symbols have been inadvisedly introduced into the cult of the Sacred Heart.

But that doesn't mean persecution doesn't exist today, openly and in hidden form. When the Holy See asked the Italian State to dismiss Professor Ernesto Bonaiuti[2], Professor of the History of Christianity at Rome University, the State bowed its head, even if Giovanni Gentile foamed at the mouth with rage - no go, the situation is catered for in an article in the Lateran Concordat between Church and State. The State should have thought of this possibility in good time. It shouldn't have let itself be tricked by negotiators in black cassocks.

Your letter must be read in this light. But allow me to dwell on the abuse of power involved in your move. I have written a book which creates unease, but it is a scientific book and the Catholic University is still a university, and recognised as such by the State. It is not a parish school. Thousands of people have graduated from it - teachers, doctors, lawyers, magistrates, businessmen, farmers and even university professors. The rules of the game compel you to refute me. The difficulty is that the brains trust specially appointed to refute Gli osservanti two years ago still hasn't been able to squeeze a single syllable out of itself.

At this point decency should have suggested you shut up. But you have preferred to resort to repression, offering my docile colleagues the opportunity to state publicly that the philosophy of law is not a scientific subject, or is, perhaps a science of a peculiar kind, where rigour of analysis, range of knowledge, and originality of thought mean nothing, and only conformity to 'Catholic principles' counts. I shudder to think what would happen if you had a free hand with culture.

My case, you tell me, has been laid before the Dean of the Faculty and the Rector. I am sure I was meant to go cold with fright when I heard that (the words growing like icicles in my mind). Your action was necessary even if unpleasant. The formula has its own cocoon - the gloomy solemnity of an irremediable decree, a court sentence, the thud of an axe falling on the block. I'm in on the secret, I know you love these things - I've read De Maistre's eulogy of the bone-smasher-cum-executioner at work on his victims strapped to the rack. Once upon a time the heretic was told to come to Rome. You pass me on to the Dean of the Faculty and the Rector, and I was meant to go and cower in a corner. The threat was useless, but must have seemed awe-inspiring to you. To judge it as it deserves, account must be taken of your mental habits. In the ecclesiastical world nothing is secure. Even the most brilliant careers are overhung by potential disaster, a rising star knows it may fall, no one trusts anyone - it's a thickly woven tangle of suspicion, rivalry, hatred, vendettas, unstable alliances falling apart as soon as they're formed and vile blows below the belt. Here's one found at random, seen face to face in your writings [3] :-

> In his very recent volume The Theory of Evolution in Science and in the Faith, the author, His Eminence Cardinal E. Ruffini states in a foreword that nearly all the book had been written by 1937. This may explain why, in explaining the position of the ecclesiastical authorities on this subject, His Eminence makes no reference to, and takes no account of, the extremely important speech made by Pius XII discussed below. This speech would, perhaps, have induced the Author to modify some of his book already in manuscript.

An absent-minded reader might slide over this passage, hearing only a pernickety archivist placing an incident in its historical setting. But anyone tuned in on the right wavelength will hear the drums of a clear accusation. How did a mere Cardinal dare to differ from the Pope?

The gravity of the charge can be gauged by comparing it with another case you discuss elsewhere. [4] The author of a theological treatise made so bold as to say it couldn't be excluded that babies dying before baptism were saved. Then Pius XII, speaking to a group of obstetricians, opted for a tough line. The theologian hurriedly cancelled that bit out of his book and jettisoned that dangerous flight of his imagination - babies who die before baptism are damned. Then Pius died and the problem became 'theologically free'. Eight years after Pius's death you write what you would never have dared to write while he was alive: that this is a difficult point, but in the end it will be decided that unbaptised babies are saved.[5]   In 1964 a breeze of theological liberalism was blowing. So why deny those poor babies the road to the heavenly gate?

It is difficult to keep your head above the waves in these seas. Nine tenths of the grey matter in the Church gets used up in the worried concentration which goes into spying on everyone else. This is a duty which every man owes it to himself to keep up, otherwise he will never survive. The top men in the hierarchy emerge from this dusky free-for-all.

In your world no one has the foggiest idea what 'respecting your neighbour's dignity' means: anonymous denunciations, evidence given in secret, sentences read without a trial, trials held without a defence, an eternally-yielding chaos which can develop rapidly to reach any conclusion. An accusation is not an accusation after all, so there's no need to formally declare innocence. But a moment later the charge is dug up and the mortal blow delivered with a lightning stroke, a model of barbarous-ness which beggars parallel. It is natural that you take these things as part of the routine, and assumed I would react as any member of your circle would in the same situation.

The Church doesn't normally use terror as an end in itself. It resorts to it reluctantly, and lets it drop at the first twitch of repentance. You are less interested in physical destruction than in the conversion of the rebel - if for no other reason than that it sets an example which more than eclipses the previous bad one. That is what you were angling for in your next phrase. You had to do your painful duty, but 'because of the respect you feel for me personally', you are ready to meet me for

a 'frank' conversation. This adjective, 'frank', occurs
with obsessive frequency in your thought, revealing a
knot in the grain of your subconscious. Who knows what
you mean by it? You have to be an expert at cracking
the code to understand these secrets. Vaticanology
and Kremlinology run parallel here. In both cases
'holding a frank exchange of views' must usually be read
as 'going for each other's throats over irreconcilable
differences'.

You can't have been expecting me to accept your
invitation, and perhaps didn't even imagine I would
answer, but you never know. If I had gone to Canossa,
the famous wind-up to Orwell's 1984 would really have
come true - the heretic starts to cry like a lambkin.
He has been naughty and deserves a punishment which
will make him an example to others. But Holy Mother
Church, out of her bottomless compassion, decides to
forgive him. You would have let me keep my job
teaching philosophy of law if I had promised to use some
ingratiating book by Don Olgiati for my course instead
of Gli osservanti. It would have been a triumph - a
heretic brought to repentance by alternating phases of
terror and forgiveness, an ideal mixture for snapping a
rebel's spine. Have you ever read, Monsignor, how
Galileo recanted?

I, Galileo, son of Vincenzo Galileo of Fiorenza,
aged seventy, called personally to judgment and
kneeling before your Eminences and Very Reverend
Cardinals, General Inquisitors in the whole of
Christendom against the wickedness of heresy;
having before my eyes the Holy Gospels, which I
touch with my hands, do swear that I have always
believed, do now believe, and, with God's help,
will always believe everything that the Holy Catholic
and Apostolic Church says, preaches and teaches.
But as I have been judged to be under strong suspicion of heresy by this Holy Court...that is, of
having thought and believed that the sun is the
centre of the world, and doesn't move, and that the

earth is not the centre and does move,...as I
want to remove from the minds of Your Eminences
and of every faithful Christian this strong suspicion,
rightly formed against me, I, with a sincere heart
and with faith which is not pretence, do recant,
·curse and loathe these errors and heresies and, in
general, all and every other error, heresy and sect
which is against the Holy Church. And I swear that
in future I will never say or assert, in speech or in
writing, things which could make anyone form sus-
picions like these against me. And if I come to know
of anyone suspected of heresy, I will denounce them
to this Holy Court or to the Inquisitor or Bishop of
the place where I am.

Recanting is not enough. You have to be a spy too.
    The Scholastic metaphysics you want to ram down
my throat is simply the longer-lived philosophical equivalent of that Ptolemaic universe which your colleagues
of 300 years ago used as a cudgel against the new astronomy. 'There can't be craters on the moon's surface -
Aristotle says that all heavenly bodies are perfect,
perfectly smooth and unchangeable. '
    This latest exercise in inquisitorial techniques is
the proof that under the smiling mask of an unpre-
judiced 'our minds are infinitely elastic' attitude, you
are the same as you always were: arrogant, power-
hungry and ruthless. Every step forward - votes and
education for everyone, the freedom of scientific
research and a civilised judicial system - has invariably
had to penetrate the barrier of your resistance, modu-
lated through every possible tone - knowing quips,
whisperings, a flow of denigration, attempts to impress
and flatter with a supposed background of non-existent
expertise, pleading with your hearts on your sleeves,
blackmail in the secrecy of the confessional, instigating
the faithful to start a Crusade...the list has only just
begun. Some energetic apologists are hard at it now,
with endless criticism of the Enlightenment, bundling
up in one short breath miniskirts, birth control and the

gas chambers at Dachau, to reach the flushed conclusion that everyone was better off in H.M.C.'s womb, in the good old days when the common people were illiterate, priests drew their tithes regularly, people obeyed without grumbling, beggars swarmed through the streets to make their benefactors feel good in unloading half-pennies, kings governed by divine right and the sight of some wretch with a body being elasticised on the rack in the city square cooled off any hot heads. I'd like to tell the truth: the attempt to free mankind is a Prome-thean task to be repeated at every opportunity, despite the clear prospect of failure, in the hope that the successive residues left by past failures will work like a yeast in society and lead to something good. There is no guarantee that this will happen and no progress can be considered permanent, because the battle is a mass of risks, and any outcome is possible, disaster included.

In this struggle you hound-dogs of orthodoxy choose the reactionary side without a flicker of hesitation, the whole bag of tricks, from Thomism in philosophy to dictatorship in politics, from pathological egging-on of unlimited population expansion to the pontifical crusade against divorce. By now, though, all that is left of your pretensions is the angry defence of the Church establish-ment. The only difference between it and the French monarchy of 1789 is that it has a network of interests and a monopoly of inertia sufficient to guarantee it a very long life. It is still strong financially, diplomatically and politically, and it has a wealth of pedagogical techniques at its disposal. But spiritually it is dying. You still have the Gospels to mouth, but inspiration has fled underground, to the small unofficial churches.

You end your letter by saying you remember me and my family in your prayers. Perhaps I ought to thank you, but I would be a hypocrite if I did. I have always hated the churchy style.

Footnotes

1. The oath sworn on 20 June 1789 by the members of

the Third Estate, which had by then proclaimed itself the National Assembly, binding it to resist the intimidations of the French Monarchy.

2. See also p. 106 f. below.
3. Scritti teologici, p. 655, note (the underlinings are mine)
4. Scritti teologici, p. 420, No. 25
5. Ibid., p. 436 f.

# THE SEQUEL

### Round One: Cardinal Garrone versus Cordero

The Church declared war on Cordero on 12 October 1970,
using Cardinal Gabriele Maria Garrone as its mouthpiece.
In Document A, Garrone's letter to Cordero, the parallel with Galileo, already suggested in Chapter XI of
this book (p.102) by Cordero, springs to urgent life
Cordero is told he must retract the main corpus of his
work - Gli osservanti, Against the Catholic System,
Breakdown Theory and his articles for the weekly
L'Espresso - the bulk of his non-technical writings then
published. And, of course, he must change his tune in
teaching. Only the purest orthodoxy, it is implied, will
be tolerated from now on. Otherwise he will lose his
job at the Catholic University of Milan.

If Italian law forbids any university to deprive a
professor of his chair and salary because of disagreement over teaching methods, even when that university
prevents him from lecturing and carrying out any of his
other duties, so much the worse. But the Catholic
University and the Church will have done their worst
against this scientific heretic.

If the wishes of the most ardent Catholic spirits
came true, Cordero would be left to starve in silence,
without, of course, being allowed the chance to publish
his books, as happened to Professor Ernesto Bonaiuti,
who lived near the starvation line for years in Mussolini's Italy, after refusing to take an oath of allegiance
to the Fascist regime. After the War, on the Church's
insistence, he was never reinstated, because Church

jurisdiction over its ex-members was one of the conditions of the Lateran Pacts, signed by Mussolini and the Vatican, and still operative today. Bonaiuti, incidentally, only survived through the support given him by his friends, none of whom were rich.

Mussolini is dead, and Italy is no longer a totalitarian country, but the Bonaiuti case gives a wealth of insight into the Catholic way of doing things, not only under Mussolini, but after the war, when the Catholics have had political as well as spiritual power.

In Cordero's case the ideological coercion could not be more explicit. If Cordero does not retract everything, the Church will withdraw its permit (nulla osta in Italian, nihil obstat in Latin) for him to teach. At all costs this disseminator of unorthodoxy must be kept away from the minds of the young. By October 1970 the Church was already well aware of the sensation caused by Against the Catholic System among students of the Catholic University, and the letter from Garrone was the first instalment of its reply. A reply not in terms of ideas or reasoning, but in the brute exercise of power.

The bare-faced presumption of the blackmail is startling. Perhaps few Catholics outside Italy are aware that such things happen in the 1970's. They may imagine that Galileo is an amusing episode in history books, that the strangling of science in the name of orthodoxy is a closed chapter of the past.

But many high-ups in the Catholic hierarchy in Italy take a different attitude - that it is bitterly to be regretted that Cordero is protected by the law from more drastic reprisals.

There has been much talk in Anglo-Saxon countries about 'the two cultures', the humanities and science. In Garrone's letter we see a third culture, an anti-culture, which, with its ideological sterility, desires to dry them up, or neutralise its two enemies.

Science or dogma? Free thought or the death-mask over orthodoxy? The same dilemmas analysed in Against the Catholic System are seen in the raw in the two documents which follow, dogmatic orthodoxy now

107

baring its snarling face against 'heterodox science'.

Document A: Letter from Cardinal Garrone to Professor
　　　　　　　Cordero

Sacra Congregatio pro Institutione Catholica, 12 October
1970
To Franco Cordero, Professor of Criminal Procedure,
Catholic University of the Sacred Heart, Milan.

Dear Professor,
This holy congregation has read your publications, both
in periodicals and in book form, appearing after the
Faculty of Law of the Catholic University had deprived
you of your professorship in the philosophy of law.

Your book Gli osservanti had contained positions
and interpretations inconsistent with profession of the
Catholic faith. Your later publications especially your
pamphlet Risposta a Monsignore (Against the Catholic
System) (De Donato, 1970) have greatly aggravated the
position. Your publications have been submitted to
competent authorities by this congregation who have
judged your position to be incompatible with that of a
lecturer in a university.

In informing you of this opinion I would like to make
known to you the full readiness of this congregation to
hold an interview with you, to discuss the questions at
issue in depth. I must also tell you that if such an interview has not taken place by the end of this month, and
if, in the absence of this interview, you have not spontaneously drawn the conclusions which inevitably follow
from the incompatibility mentioned above, this congregation must proceed to carry out its duty - it must, that
is, revise the initially positive judgment formed about
you when a permit (nulla osta) was given to your
appointment as Professor of Criminal Procedure at the
Catholic University of the Sacred Heart. The validity of
this permit must now lapse.

I await your decisions and send my respects,
                    Cardinal Garrone
                    Giuseppe Schröffer, Secretary


Document B: Cordero's Reply to Cardinal Garrone
            Published in L'Espresso, 1 November 1970

Your Eminence,
To someone in the dark about ecclesiastical phenomena,
your letter might give the profoundly mistaken impression
of being 'autistic'. As you know, this neologism by
Eugen Bleuler describes the attitude of people who live
outside reality: a 'holy congregation' notes down every
syllable which comes from my pen, Gli osservanti
deserves the adjective heterodox - and my later work
has 'greatly aggravated' the position; 'competent
authorities' give out their judgment that opinions of that
cut are incompatible with holding a university chair;
either I put in an appearance in Rome by 31 October to
hear your holy words and eclipse every one of mine in
a global recant, following a formula it would be your
pleasure to model to the case, or I can say goodbye to
my job. As a professor, my mouth will be shut.
        Similar treatment was given to William Occam,
summoned from Oxford to Avignon to offer his excuses
for fifty-six heresies pincered out of his commentary to
Peter Lombard's Sentenze; and he can hardly have
enjoyed it. But 645 years of history have not been a
complete blank. Two kings have lost their heads - one
rolled in England, one in France. Astronomy and
genetics are no longer developed by digging into the
Bible. Stakes have been extinguished. Holy Mother has
even swallowed working-class education - until a very
few years ago considered an invention of the devil. Most
important of all, professors - even at a Catholic University - hesitate to step beyond one limit, that of
scientific decency. And no one - police chiefs, Ministers,
bishops, or holy congregations - asserts the right to

remove them from their posts for crimes of thought.

Is your letter a jump back into the past? Half an hour's hallucination? No, that's what frightens me. The Church can be accused of almost everything, but not of being soft in the head. Its worldly experience makes every other kind of worldly wisdom look insignificant.

Its rule is never disturbed by hesitation. It raises certain types of individual, crushes others. And calculates, cold-bloodedly, where laymen would go wild. Has no feelings - discards them as useless - but pours them in torrents into its flocks. Follows its vendettas up through vast cycles of time. Absorbs everything. Is not queasy over inhuman methods. Turns chameleon wherever interest demands. Has been preaching full spate the foulness of women and their bodies, bags of filth, from St. Jerome on. (It had its own excellent reasons.) But the moment it saw sex as a prop to ecclesiastical power, we would hear the erogenous zones of women's bodies being harped on in the hushed music of delicate sermons '.

An extremely grave development, then. You weighed your words, raked the facts over, scrutinised the future, mapped out the moment, warmed up the precedents. You knew I would refuse. You know as well as I do that a man cannot be deprived of his Chair at a Catholic University any more than he can at a State one. At least as long as the Catholic University expects to be recognised by the State. If, despite all this, you sent off your letter, that means you were sure of yourselves. Like bridge, when a dour player sends shivers of ice running down his opponents' spines by announcing a fantastic bid.

High stakes are on the table. The reputation of being unbeatable is indispensable to an institution whose doctrines shatter at the first explosion of facts. Its intellectual and moral weaknesses are notorious, but everyone pretends they don't exist, because priests are power - perhaps the only type worth the name. They have developed the theory and practice of power worked in its pure state to a peak of perfection.

Priests clap appalled admiration into the crowd - just as savages are thunderstruck by animal symbols of God, like Leviathan, the monstrous sea-going crocodile in the Book of Job. Anguish is felt at the thought of having them as enemies. Besides, what they yield as friends! That's why the Church has more use for mock laymen than for spanielly bootlickers. Priests and sham laymen hatch a thousand forms of unpublicised gain between them. The two types transmit, quiet as telepathy. The dewy eyes of believers, fogged by glutinous sentiment, end up by nauseating their masters. The starry eyed are worth no more to them than stray dogs. Offer a bone and hundreds come flocking in.

Your letter, Eminence, has started a struggle which will keep both sham laymen and simpering believers breathless[2]. Especially the first: they are able to instantaneously decipher the most trivial events, symbols in the code of power. The moment has been chosen with care. Lay-party rebels who secrete their sympathies[3], ultras bellowing with rage, and the frenzied wait to see what tricks the Catholic imagination would pull out of its ample sleeves in the Lower House.

'A jurist, a man without protectors, and impudent enough to attack Holy Mother! Scribble a few books to liquidate 2000 years of wisdom? Not enough, by my estimate. What's he written? I don't know - couldn't care. Can't even be called courage - suicidal childishness. What has She done, the Great Saviour? Nothing extraordinary. She let him talk away. The supernatural chooses its own moment for revenge. When she was sure the time was ripe - a snap of her fingers, and she snuffed him out. What's happened to him now, you say? I couldn't care less.' Those will be the thoughts of 'balanced minds' if your piece of religious policing has the desired effect. And if...better not disturb one's brain. But Italian society is quaking with explosive upwellings; a keyboard of tremors running from divorce to the State-Church Lateran Concordat.

If I can hazard an opinion I would say yours is the

risk of a gambler rather than the sure-fire choice of a
subtle politician. You have unleashed a case in which
the Catholic University is wallowing up to its neck:
is its statute compatible with Italian law? And its
methods of indoctrination? Its role as incubator of a
coarse class of domineering politicians? Is it a university at all, this place of no doubt, no doubt that the
teachings of the revered elders of the church are
'externally-operative prohibitive norms for the study of
history as for any other kind of rational research'. The
'Pope's theologian' lit that cracker without a quiver of
discomfort.) You have raised these already high seas
further in a situation full of future possibilities and
open to any solution.

But you are past masters in political calculation,
and I wouldn't like to insist. If, after going over all
your calculations, you made your move, I take it you
had plenty to go on. Each side will play its cards. The
scores will be added up at the end. Scores consisting of
facts and situations: on the intellectual, moral and
aesthetic planes the game has already been played out,
and all the results are known. Even a superficial
observer realises that your move is important not so
much for the immediate results you hope to get out of
it, as for its intended function as the first in a series
meant to swell much wider. Today we will immobilise
a professor in our ectoplasm, tomorrow a whole
society. The same kind of relationship as that between
the exploit of the Condor legion in wiping Guernica off
the map, and the successive years of massacre dropped
from Fascist planes in the Spanish Civil war.

Now, to answer you point by point. I never doubted
my writings were followed in high places. When an
empire is at stake, insomniac guardians are found. I
once lived under the supervision of one who would enjoy
picking heresies out of the most reputable of the Gospels.
What surprises me is the localisation of the area under
inspection, and, therefore, the inevitable blast of
anathema. Your wording is unclear, but you seem to

be referring first to Gli osservanti[4], and then to everything published after 1 December 1969[5] - Risposta a
Monsignore, Trattato di decomposizione[6] and articles
published in L'Espresso. Must I deduce that the material
published in between - Genus[7] and Lutero contro Erasmo[8],
is impeccable Catholicism? Whatever the answer, the
problem is a brain teaser of little practical importance.
The needles on the dial of theological inquisition swing
as the operator decides. With equal plausibility, de Sade
could be canonised and St. Thomas Aquinas put on the
Index.

To come to the crux of your charge. Gli osservanti
was a disquieting book; the later ones, especially
Risposta a Monsignore (Against the Catholic System)
'have greatly aggravated the position'.
    The reply to the first point comes by itself. Gli
osservanti is a book of science. Almost 700 pages dissect
mankind as a species which produces and absorbs norms.
The clinical material is gathered from a variety of sources:
Greek mythology, theological diatribes, political tracts
and so on. The type of analysis varies too, from case
to case, in the attempt to straighten out syntax and
uncover the facts as they were before an inventive streak
got to work on them.
    A book like this cannot be recommended as enter-
tainment for fogged minds or weak stomachs. A sharp-
pointed drill will split too many nerves in a subject
mined with buried interests. Some people spin out of
control. Stripping the lustrous gleam off time-honoured
relics, to show an uninviting reality, is the kind of
subversion which entails professional risks.
    But in a university worth the name it is a professor's
duty to give - and a student's right to expect - something
better than the usual watery gruel. At least, if there's
anything alive in his head. Whether or not this activity
nourishes 'profession of the Catholic faith' is a question
which has no business intruding here. Orthodoxy is a
poor debater. Scientific hypotheses must be ground to
perfection in the light of experience and logic.

You considered my book a provocation? You should either have refuted it or steeled your minds to accepting it - if you had been willing to play fair. (Faith, decapitated of its myths, would thrive, not wilt) But no. The cannibals of Catholicism, who have incisors as sharp as wild beasts when they use them in pious denigration, turn out to be as harmless as new-born babes in the scientific field. The brains trust appointed three years ago to chaw me to a pulp is still straining to get its first word out. Instead, the 'Pope's theologian' put pen to paper and produced a remarkable letter, the gist of which was 'Any intelligent student who reads Gli osservanti will lose his faith'. In any other human environment a perpetrator of a gaffe of this enormity would immediately be put out of harm's way. But you prized his effort. I had the nerve to answer him in public. So here's the holy congregation to the rescue. 'You roughed up Monsignor in a pamphlet, did you? You were forgetting he had us behind him. Now you'll pay for it all.' The same narcissistic logic that you always apply: the supernatural chooses its own methods for revenge.

This tableau is a perfect illustration of how thoroughly ecclesiastical high-ups are immunised against psychological reactions which would floor any layman. Shame, for one.

Risposta a Monsignore (it is my pleasure, by the way, to announce a future English-language edition) is a book which many found irritating. It discussed the way logic is massacred in theology and how Father Gemelli's apologetics depend on paranoiac mechanisms, to give two examples.

After I had roused your fury thus far, Eminence, can you imagine how the bloodhounds of orthodoxy would have torn me limb from limb if I had stepped just one inch beyond the truth? (They would have done it, of course, in the name of Catholic morality) Haven't you been told, Eminence, how they reacted? Stony, appalled silence. Like insects, which freeze in feigned death, to save themselves from extreme danger.

The Rector sent me a letter of tight-lipped disapproval.
He had read, he said, only the last chapter, which
appeared as a pre-publication excerpt in L'Espresso.
'I will not attempt to pass judgment on your behaviour.
I leave that to every person of good sense.' You,
Eminence, know what kind of psychological Grand
Guignol swarms under the banner 'Catholic good sense.'
Anyway, if I can judge by the reception given to my book
in Italy and abroad, the world is full of people deprived
of it.

Monsignor has had to make do with a long overdue,
grammatically insecure routine defence[9] knocked together by a personal dependant (a 'left-wing Catholic'!).
I searched unsuccessfully for some trace of a reply to
the main ideas expressed in the book. Instead, an
unexpected defence of Gemelli. I had cited an article
written in August 1924 which expanded the delicate
thought that

> If not only positivism, but socialism and free-
> thinking, too - if not only Momigliano, but all Jews,
> people carrying on the work of the Jews who cruci-
> fied our Lord - if they all died, wouldn't the world
> be a better place?

as evidence of the insatiable aggression of that openly
Fascist priest. Back comes the reply - that wasn't an
article, it was a short contribution, dash it!

In a situation like that a layman would try to get
off the subject. But here I have your letter telling me
that my book has 'greatly aggravated' the position. All
sins are candidates for mercy, except one - the stubborn
habit of telling the truth. My writings have been submitted to 'competent authorities', who now brandish
their judgment: my position is incompatible with my
profession, that of 'a university lecturer'.

Am I wrong, or are your repressive moves being
sabotaged by a wicked imp who prompts amazing gaffes?
First Monsignor issued his oracular judgment that no
intelligent student could read Gli osservanti without

losing his Catholic faith. Now here is a Cardinal forgetting to distinguish between a Catholic University (the only State-recognised one in Italy) and all the lay universities in this country. Have all the latter been shunted into the former in your mind? The tragic thing is, you are not far wrong.

A professor you approve of does not follow up unhealthy curiosity. He receives time-worn formulae from other generations, brushes them up and passes them on. He does not read Freud, Nietzsche or Carnap. Or even the medieval theologians. The only new things about his books are paper and cover. The product of little thought - none at all, on close examination.

His work is different - trafficking among his buddies, raking money out of every corner, reverencing authority in all its forms - he would chop himself into eight if that would win its approval.

A man like that would never have had the insolence to go rummaging around in the Vajont trial[10], in the Valpreda case[11], in the malfunctioning of Italian justice or in the spirit of reaction as it appears in Italy, marinated for four centuries in the essence of the Counter-Reformation. Nor would he have written a portrait gallery of twenty-five human types affected by the psychopathology of power - a cross-section of my daily experience. How does a level-headed Italian don behave? Exactly as the professors of geology behaved at the first Vajont trial, radiating scientific glory by asserting that landslides are utterly unpredictable. Mountains sometimes move and sometimes don't.

I have to admit it - you're right. As an Italian professor I'm the wrong type. My six books on criminal procedure are appreciated by experts, but that doesn't count. My spirit of pigheaded independence has ruined me. At forty-two I'm still almost young, but in my eleven years as professor I've seen too much.

Just think, your Eminence, I haven't gone to elect the members of examining boards for new university appointments for years. That shows how little the power struggle interests me. The Law Faculty has its own mafia, nine-tenths of it Catholic, who consider me a living provocation. The new generation know they mustn't mention my name. One man has increased his popularity by handing out libere docenze[12] to candidates who had been failed by me, on the fine principle that libere docenze should never be refused - at least, not to your friends, your friends' friends, or your enemies' enemies.

Then you tell me about 'the full readiness of this holy congregation to hold an interview with you, to discuss the questions at issue in depth'. I wouldn't want to appear rude. But what should we talk about? Magic in the sacraments measured on Mauss's standards? - how the dogma of the Trinity grew out of nothing? - the smoke-screens whirling round natural law? - the fascism of Father Gemelli? - the models of morality held up for the admiration of students at the Catholic University? - the sins of being intelligent? - or what?

The interview might seem attractive as offering material for a literary portrait. But I haven't got the high-pitched subtlety needed for tricks at that level. Besides, my own experience plus my imagination give me quite enough to go on. So an experiment in vivo isn't the right bait to get me to Rome.

Anyway, why should I go to an interview whose con-clusions have already been fixed by yourself? You tell me that. Either I show up in Rome before 1 November, or 'spontaneously draw the conclusions which inevitably follow from the incompatibility mentioned above'. If not, the holy congregation will withdraw its permit allowing me to lecture at the Catholic University, which 'must now lapse'. Your 'interview in depth' would be an order to recant.

You say you look forward to hearing my decisions. I won't disappoint you. I will go on the same as ever - thinking, talking and writing. Every time I have to choose between self-respect and obedience to a power-wielder, I'll tell the power-wielder to go to hell. And every time I have a chance to encourage a taste for moral courage and blunt truth in another person, I won't miss it. I don't want to sound the least boastful - God knows the sadness I feel at having to put these thoughts into words.

I must also state explicitly why I am not giving up my Chair, even if my reasons are already implicit in what I have written. There are three.

First, my Chair was not a present from a friendly bishop or a holy congregation. I sweated for it. I earned it with thousands of pages from my own brain.

Second, I rebut the charge of inconsistency. I would like to know how I should describe the presumption of the authorities in running a State-recognised university as if it was a parish church. The day the State's recognition of the Catholic University of Milan 'lapses', I'll go. Till then I have the right to be treated as a regularly-appointed professor. If I went it would be taken as a tacit admission that the University authorities, egged on by the 'Pope's theologian', are entitled to lay down the law on what is true and false in science - which is not only bizarre, but gross. Sometimes 'co-operation' is the easiest way out, but the shabbiest.

Third, I wouldn't be out of range of moral thuggery at any other Italian university. Holy Mother's arms stretch far. The incense-bearers of power thrive at all latitudes.

Your withdrawal of your nulla osta is your own business. But I will react if anyone tries to seize my university Chair. There are laws in Italy, and judges. A case on this question would be the best possible way of seeing whether Italy is a democratic republic or a papal feud.

I am sorry if this letter hasn't come up to your expectations.

I send you my respects.

Franco Cordero

## Round Two: The Vatican versus Cordero

If the Church had showed the face of repression in Garrone's letter, there was a certain minimum of decorum in, let us say, the presentation. Along with the elegant headed notepaper, the blackmail was phrased in what sounds like 'civilised language'.

With Document C we sink to a still lower level. To add the final touch, this extraordinary piece of lying appeared in L'Osservatore Romano, the official Vatican newspaper.

The article asserted that Cordero had misreported the text of Garrone's letter. Where the text of the letter stated that no such person as Cordero should teach in any university, Cordero (it asserted) had altered this from any Catholic university by omitting the word 'Catholic' when publishing Garrone's letter (my underlining).

The idiotic baseness of producing a lie of this order is indeed staggering. It might seem inexplicable. But there the fact stands. The original of the letter is in Cordero's possession, and when L'Espresso published Garrone's letter and Cordero's reply, the former was reprinted from a photocopy. It is scientifically certain that the only falsification is that by the Vatican newspaper.

Why should the Vatican stoop to such infantile trickery? There was one compelling reason. The Church had been unable to reply with arguments or debate either to Gli osservanti or to Riposta a Monsignore or to any of Cordero's other writings. It had been incapable of producing a word against them, and now, after more than one and a half years, in 1972, its silence is still total. Slander - however superficial, however easily unmasked - must have seemed the only way to damage his reputation.

Maybe the calculation was superficial. Maybe this book will conclude that the reputation that has been damaged is that of the Vatican, while that of Cordero has grown with his reply. The verdict lies with the reader.

Postscript for Catholics.  Someone wishing to defend
the Vatican over documents A and C could, at this point,
advance only one hypothesis, that Cordero had forged
the entire document.  If the Vatican had believed that,
it was its clear duty and in its own interest to take
Cordero to court on charges of slander, ideological
misrepresentation (falso ideologico) and forgery of a
document presented as genuine.

No illusions are possible.  The proofs of authenticity
are 100 per cent.

Any Catholic should feel deeply disturbed.  Nothing
could have been more eloquent than the total silence
which has followed this incident.  The legal silence has
echoed and reinforced the ideoglogical one.


Document C:  Article published in the Vatican newspaper
              L'Osservatore Romano, 1 November 1970

The Holy Congregation for Catholic Education wrote to
Professor Cordero on 12 October 1970, telling him,
among other things, that, 'Your publications have been
submitted to competent authorities by this congregation,
who have judged your position to be incompatible with
that of a lecturer in a Catholic University. '

Professor Cordero has had this letter published by
L'Espressò (Year 14, no. 44, p. 10), mutilating it,
however, by omitting a word which is essential to the
meaning of the letter from the Holy Congregation.
Cordero left out the adjective 'Catholic' before 'university'

Cordero, basing his argument on a letter he has
wilfully falsified in this way, asserts 'You, Eminence,
forget to distinguish between a Catholic University (the
only state-recognised one in Italy) and all the lay universities in the country'.

This is one of the basic arguments in Cordero's
reply published in L'Espresso.

Any comment appears superfluous. Methods like these seem irreconcilable with the truth, which Cordero says he fights for at all costs.

Document D: Letter by Franco Cordero, published in L'Espresso in reply to article in L'Osservatore Romano.

To Cardinal Gabriele Maria Garrone,
Eminence, in answering your letter I remarked that the Catholic Church has a formidable grip on reality. But new developments supply evidence for the other hypothesis - that you were using language autistically. Sometimes people talk and gesticulate as if wanting something hard enough was the way of getting it.

The Osservatore Romano of 1 November accuses me of 'mutilating' your letter. You, it says, wrote that my position was incompatible with that of a lecturer in a Catholic university, and I, it goes on, left out the word 'Catholic' - 'which is essential to the meaning of the letter from the Holy Congregation'.

By basing my arguments on a text I had 'wilfully falsified in this way', I had, therefore, made things easy for myself. 'Any comment appears superfluous', the article concludes with self-satisfaction, 'Methods like these seem irreconcilable with the truth, which Cordero says he fights for at all costs'.

At first, I'm afraid, I was taken aback. Could that letter have really contained that adjective which some kind of a spell had stopped me seeing? But no, I told myself, I had read it over and over again, and I hadn't been the only one. Besides, the text of the letter as it appeared in L'Espresso came from a photo of the original. Superstitious fear can flare up even in a mind hardened by sacrilegious irony.

But I only had to pick up the letter and hold it up to the light to exorcise this ghost. Not even the shadow of the word 'Catholic' was there beside 'university'. It was a pleasure to see causal relationships stand firm. Facts are facts and nouns aren't adjectives, even for a mere layman like myself, and even when face to face with a Prince of the Church, like yourself. There is at least one corner of reality which doesn't yield to your charismatic powers.

After this metaphysical investigation had come to a happy ending, a moral question sprang to mind. The official Vatican newspaper had falsely accused me of falsifying a letter. It had distorted the truth in a bare-faced and poisonously slanderous way.

But what would be the point of arguing with a faithful scribe? If you had been told to write that my letter didn't exist, that's what you would have written. And if they tell you tomorrow to praise me to the skies as a paragon of Catholic virtue, that's what you will do.

As far as I know the Osservatore Romano has never published a correction. Everything printed there is 24-carat gold. Even if it was announced one day that the Straits of Magellan didn't exist, it would stand as the truth for all time. ('The Case of the Missing Adjective' is the same thing in reverse.) So I prefer to leave the Vatican newspaper to its own devices, and talk about you, Eminence. Only three hypotheses could excuse you: someone in your retinue stabbed you in the back; you signed the letter without reading it; your memory slipped you.

The letter as it is signed states that my position is incompatible with that of a university lecturer, without further proviso. Was the lacuna intentional? Priests choose their words carefully. There was a reason for not inserting the word 'Catholic'. If scientific truths which you are incapable of refuting must not be heard within the Catholic University, then that institution is not a university as defined by the Italian Constitution. Experts in Canon Law are hardly likely to have diffi-culty over interpreting Article 33 of the Constitution, which reads:

Art and Science are free, and so is the teaching of these subjects.

And Article 4 of Law 311, 18 March 1958, adds:

> All teachers are guaranteed freedom in teaching
> and scientific research.

If you are going against the Italian Constitution and the
Laws of Italy, why not go the whole hog, and label me
as unfit to teach in a 'university' in general - certainly
a more sinister phrase? Finally, the psychological
angle must not be overlooked. Taken literally your
phrase expresses, with the inevitability of a compulsive
gesture, your nostalgia for the good old days when Holy
Mother was the one to make laws, not obey them.

I had also, if you remember, wondered if there
mightn't be a wicked imp at work, sabotaging your repression by prompting you to amazing gaffes.

Someone brought up on Aeschylus would call in fate to
explain these things. But a practitioner in social psychology would compile a list of six classic features of
ecclesiastical behaviour, as I have done:

1. A free run for fantasy.

The mental addition of an adjective which had been un-
ceremoniously left out, and now has to be put back, is
not a surprising quirk in someone employed to juggle
daily with the supernatural.

2. Immorality.

It's one thing to be carried away by flights of the mind,
another to alter the past in cold blood. People of the
first type are innocents, or, in desperate cases, mytho-
maniacs; those in the second, common forgers.

3. Shamelessness.

The person who planned that little coup in L'Osservatore
Romano knew the effect would wear off quickly - it could
only last as long as it took to unmask. The fact that he
still decided to set the mechanism in motion shows the
depth of his contempt for public opinion.

4. Aggressiveness.

The Catholic University is unable to react on the plane
of intellectual argument, so it proceeds to discredit me
- in the eyes of the faithful, at least. And here is the
gleeful executioner letting himself go with his traditional
mockery of fair play, chanting that I 'wilfully falsify'
letters by cardinals.

5. <u>Coarse jeering</u>.

The reprobate must be wiped off the moral scene. The
attaché in this holy work of justice spits in his face after
the axe has fallen. In fact, after the exquisitely slanderous
fairy story of the doctored letter, a leering comment
prints its moral: 'Methods like these seem irreconcilable
with the truth, which Cordero says he fights for at all
costs.'

6. <u>The subintellectual tone of the attack</u>.

Distortion of the truth as crass as this could only make
the authorities cut a worse figure. A subtler polemicist
would have written, 'In writing "university" I obviously
meant "Catholic University"'. I had expected that sort
of reply, and so hadn't laboured the point. But I was
overestimating the intellectual powers of my opponents,
as sometimes happens. I understand now why the 'Pope's
theologian' wants to vaccinate students at the Catholic
University against ideas.

I send you my respects,

Franco Cordero

Footnotes

1. A flurry of experimental 'beat' Communions have
   been tried on, ploughing through a flap of flustered
   opinion. Women, Paul VI has now ruled, can read
   the lesson and lead the responses, but cannot be
   allowed anywhere near the altar.
       Allowing sex into Catholicism may seem a wild
   dream. But some English Catholics, eager to appear
   modern, risked their hides by speaking in favour of

D.H. Lawrence at the time of the trial over the un-
abridged edition of Lady Chatterley's Lover. Lawrence
reeks of sex swooning into religion. There's nothing
inherently impossible about making religion swoon
into sex. A more modern version of the practices
of Mme. Guyon would be needed. (Translator)

2. It may interest readers to know that, since the
Vatican article of 1 November 1970 in L'Osservatore
Romano (Document C), the Church has not ventured
into print. Cordero has published Le masche (his
second novel: Rizzoli, Milan, 1971), L'Epistola ai
Romani (an analysis of St. Paul's Epistle to the
Romans: Einaudi, Turin, 1972) and Opus (his third
novel: Einaudi, Turin, 1972). He contributes regularly to L'Espresso. For previous publications see
p. 16 and notes 4, 6, 7, 8, 10 below.

3. After all the senators had expressed their voting
intentions on the Baslini-Fortuna Divorce Bill
(October 1970), the pro-divorce senators should have
had a majority of at least fourteen. On a vote camou-
flaged as a motion to postpone discussion, fourteen
inexplicably sank to two: sure evidence of secret
pacts and sympathies. (In Italy parliamentary voting
is secret.)

   The Bill, which was sponsored by the (right-wing)
Liberals and (left-wing) Socialists, was supported by
all the lay parties except the Neo-Fascists and
Monarchists. These joined the Christian Democrats
in opposing it.

   Since the Bill became law there have been cease-
less manoeuvres to destroy it, either by repealing it
through a general referendum or by watering it down
in a 'compromise' bill. (Translator)

4. Gli osservanti, Giuffre, Milan, 1967.

5. The date on which Cordero was deprived of his professorship in the philosophy of law. See the opening
sentence of Garrone's letter. (Translator)

6. De Donato, Bari, 1970. Breakdown Theory: a
stinging analysis of religious superstition, Cordero's
most ambitious study in depth of religious belief.
(Translator)

7. De Donato, Bari, 1969. Cordero's first novel; it won the Viareggio Prize in 1969. (Translator)
8. De Donato, Bari, 1969. Luther versus Erasmus: contrasts the intellectual courage of Luther with the finely calculated conformism of Erasmus, usually lionised as a liberal humanist. (Translator)
9. Published as a review of Risposta a Monsignore in the Catholic weekly Settegiorni, six months late. (Translator)
10. The Vajont Dam, the highest in Europe, broke on 9 November 1963, after enormous masses of water had been displaced by a landslide. 1,994 people in the valley below were killed. After a re-trial (1970) the final sentence condemned the accused directors of the SADE company (who had repeatedly ignored warnings of disaster, even while one side of the mountain was in movement; and had actually raised the water level only months before) of wilful negligence, and as being personally responsible for the homicide of 1,994 people. But the longest sentence was six years.

    A long article by Cordero in Espresso-Colore, 26 July 1970, described the irresponsibility of power, judicial complicity, the role of money, and the indifference to the population of the valley. (Translator)
11. Immediately after the Milan bomb outrage in December 1969 (sixteen people killed) the anarchist Pietro Valpreda was arrested. The case against him rests almost entirely on the evidence of a taxi-driver, who was shown a photo of Valpreda before being asked to identify him (suitably unshaven, after days of prison, among four spruce plain-clothes policemen). An abortive preliminary trial, which started on 23 February 1972, was abandoned after ten days. (In Italy there is no limit to the time an accused person may spend in prison before trial. Half of those found guilty immediately leave prison, because they have served their sentence awaiting trial. Those found innocent must consider themselves lucky to have been tried and acquitted.) Cordero's article

first appeared in L'Espresso on 4 October 1970. (Translator)

12. Research degrees. A libera docenza is the first big landmark in a university career. It is a professional qualification, not an appointment. The second is a Chair, which is both.

   This whole system would have been changed by the University Reform Bill, which has been in preparation for four years, and going through Parliament for two. But, like Beckett's Godot its meaning lies in being waited for. (Translator)

# NOTES

Brief notes on historical personalities and a few technical terms

**ALACOQUE** St. Marguerite Marie (1647-1690). Cured of paralysis at an early age. Put this down to direct intercession by the Virgin. Took vows in 1672. After a long period of self-deprivation said Christ had revealed his Holy Heart to her, and had told her to institute the 'Holy Hour' (act of grace guaranteed to anyone going to Communion on first Fridays of nine consecutive months). Cult of Sacred Heart spread like wildfire through Europe. After some delay protests very gradually started to roll in from Jansenists, specially Scipio de Ricci, Bishop of Pistoia. But Pope Pius VII condemned Jansenists in 1794 in his Bull Auctorem Fidei (1794), and de Ricci submitted in 1805.

**AVERROES** (1126-1198). Greatest Arab philosopher in West. Made his reputation as commentator on Aristotle. Was given so many important jobs in Spain (Judge of Seville, 1169; later in Cordoba) he complained he had no time left for philosophy. The common people started getting suspicious of theoretical science, and Averroes spent much of his old age under house arrest. This backlash of ignorance led to collapse of Arab science after he died. His doctrines lived on chiefly in the minds of the Latin Averroists in Paris, who said 'God eternally produces the intelligence by emanation. Matter is eternal potency. The active intellect is one and the same for everyone. There is no freedom or personal immortality. There are contradictions between religion and philosophical truth.'

**ALBIGENSIANS** (or **ALBIGENSES**). Lived in South-East France and developed the Provençal civilization (made famous in English by Ezra Pound with his Provençal reconstructions and Cantos). Their religion was Catharism. Not much is known about it because every trace of this

noble people was wiped out after an investigation by
Innocent II turned into the quickest, largest-scale, most
bloodthirsty general slaughter technically conceivable
at the time. Robert le Bourgre directed the operation
personally.' What is known is that the Albigensian
people loved the Cathars, that the Cathars taught a
personal religion of the heart (without hierarchies of
priests), that the princes in the area supported them,
that even the official Catholic bishops in the area refused
to do anything against them, that their art and culture
was of a staggeringly high level (certainly much higher
than that of their murderers), and that the Church wasn't
content till a whole civilisation had been wiped off the
map and - as far as humanly possible - out of human
knowledge.

ARNALDO DA BRESCIA. Italian political reformer.
Lived in France during youth. Follower of Abelard. On
getting back to Italy formed powerful group preaching
against corruption of clergy. Wanted to guide Church
back to original simplicity of early Christianity. First
result of his work was revolt of the people of Brescia
against their bishop. Under accusation at Council of
Latran (1139), Arnaldo had to promise Innocent II he
would keep quiet. Went back to France to work with
Abelard. Both of them were condemned by Council of
Sens in 1140. Arnaldo took refuge in Switzerland, with
Bishop of Constance, and went back to Italy after death
of Innocent II. His supporters called him to Rome in
1145.

He forced Pope Eugene III to leave Rome. With the
support of aristocracy and people took on job of re-
establishing civil liberty and reforming clergy. He set
up a Senate, Tribunal and equestrian order.

In 1155 Hadrian IV placed a religious ban on Rome.
The Romans were horrified, and exiled Arnaldo. He
was soon handed over to the Pope's supporters, thanks
to the intervention of Frederick Barbarossa. Was taken
to Rome and strangled by order of the Prefect. Body
burned and ashes thrown in Tiber. Contemporary

writers, even St. Bernard, testified to his remarkable talents and uncanny eloquence, and all acknowledged great purity of his morals.

BASIL, St. (330-379). Bishop of Caesarea. Appointed in 370. The Encyclopaedia Britannica lets loose some unconscious irony when it states objectively 'his great powers were called into action to stamp out Arians... [he was] hot-blooded and imperious'.

BELLARMINO (1532-1621). (English writers often anglicize this name to 'Bellarmine').
The most important of Galileo's prosecutors.

CASUIST. One who specialises in Christian moral theology, discussing all possible sides of questions of uncertain morality. Originally a term invented by the common people in reacting against finicky reasoning used to drag out ludicrous conclusions (they considered this subversive of true morality and a vile exercise in priest-craft). Now a term accepted by the Church itself.

CLOVIS (466-511). King of the Franks. Founder of Merovingian Empire in Europe. Career consisted mainly of wars, murders and intrigues. Wife Clotilda an ardent Catholic. Gregory of Tours gives detailed account of Clovis's conversion, which resulted in colossal territorial gains for the Church.

CONSTANS I, Flavius Julius. (320 or 323-350). Roman Emperor. Protector of Nicene Creed. Youngest son of Constantine I and Fausta. After death of father divided Empire up with his two brothers, Constantine II and Constantius II, getting Italy, Africa and Illyricum as his share. His misrule led to insurrections everywhere. Fled to Spain, but was overtaken at foot of Pyrenees and killed.

GEMELLI, Father Agostino (1878-1959). Founded Catholic University of the Sacred Heart, Milan, 1921.

Rector of the University from its foundation. Founder of the Rivista di filosofia neoscolastica ('Review of Neo-scholastic Philosophy'), and of Vita e pensiero ('Life and Thought'), in 1914, together with Don Olgiati and V. Necchi. Founder of Archivio di psicologia, neurologia e psichiatria, 1922.

GIANNONE, Pietro (1676-1784). Neapolitan historian. Chief work is Civil History of the Kingdom of Naples (1723) which led to his excommunication. He took refuge in Geneva. Once took the risk of going into Savoy and was immediately seized by Sardinian police. Put in the fortress-prison of Turin. Recanted, but was not released. Died there.

GILSON, Etienne (born 1884). Catholic philosopher. Chief aim has been to place Catholic doctrines firmly within framework of Middle Ages and to prove medieval philosophy still plays a vital role in modern knowledge.

GUYON, Mme Jeanne-Marie (1648-1717). French mystic. Left a widow at 24. After fixing up a marriage between her daughter and superintendent Fouquet, which assured her excellent relations at Court, went to live in Paris. Claimed she had experienced direct union with God and consequent ecstasy. Her doctrines stirred up a welter of controversy. She found a staunch admirer in Mme. de Maintenon, but a running duel developed between Bossuet, backed up Louis XIV, who had lost patience with Mme. Guyon, and Fénelon, who supported her. Louis was the strongest combatant, and Mme. Guyon was left to cool off in prison at Vincennes, and later in the Bastille. Freed in 1702. She died after submitting to the Church. After her death her rehabilitation became almost complete.

HEGEL, Georg Wilhelm Friedrich (1770-1831). Extremely important German 'Idealist' philosopher (not idealist in an English sense). Founded his philosophy on acceptance of the facts as they are, exalted the historical process as a kind of evolutionary development of humanity, singled out World Historical Figures who were supposed to have grasped and personified the spirit of the age - what the age 'demanded'. Said 'Reason is a Bacchanalian feast at which all the guests are drunk' and justified wars and violence as 'the slaughter-bench of history' Gave rise to two main German schools, of right-wing Hegelians, who accepted the status quo as the perfect achievement of history and the left-wing Hegelians, who wanted to accelerate and develop the dynamics of history, so superseding the status quo.

KELSEN, Hans, (born 1881). Probably the greatest jurist of this century. Founder of the 'pure theory' of law. For instance, the State, from a legal point of view, must be considered a system of norms the citizen is legally constrained to obey, not a spiritual entity which has the right to claim an unlimited range of unspecified allegiance. Author of important books on International Law and the General Theory of Law. Born in Prague, but emigrated first to Switzerland, then to U.S.A., where he taught at Harvard and at University of California. In maturity has written on sociology.

KLEIN, Melanie (1882-1960). Pioneer in field of infant psychology. Invented technique of making children play games to understand their psychology. Has been called the only revolutionary force in psychology since Freud. Was born in Vienna, but moved to London in 1926.

LOMBARD, Peter (Pietro Lombardo; c.1100-c.1160). Bishop of Paris. Knocked together a personal collection of the views of the Church fathers - Sententiarum libri quatuor, which became virtually de rigueur in theological colleges all over Europe. Chief innovation was the explicit claim the sacraments were not just 'a sign of grace' but a medium for its actual on-site transference.

LYSENKO. Russian biologist. Under Stalin occupied position of great power. No one was allowed to argue

with him or his theories - with disastrous results for
Russian science.

NIETZSCHE, Friedrich (1844-1900). A brilliant,
erratic, unconventional, visionary philosopher whose
chief targets were squashy (sentimental) Christianity
and the middle classes. He claimed to follow in a tradition of thought running through the pre-Socratic philosophers (Heraklitus, Empedocles), the figure of Kallikles
as he appears in Plato's Gorgias, Spinoza, and Goethe.
He died raving. A lot of his work was published in
adulterated form by his widowed sister Elizabeth Förster-
Nietzsche to give it an anti-Jewish slant. Many people
now consider Nietzsche a forerunner of the Frankfurt
School (Marcuse, Horkheimer, Adorno), prophesying
the disintegration of individual personality and an ever-
widening gap between the inspired 'tight-rope walkers'
responsible for mankind's destiny and the characterless,
smooth-running cogs owned by the system. He despised
the university system as a tamer of knowledge - 'The
State's only interest in universities is to produce obedient,
servile citizens'.

OCCAM (or OCKHAM), William (c.1290-1349). One of
the most brilliant and laughably underrated figures in
English philosophy. Acknowledged by Luther as 'my
master'. Developed Scholasticism along his own lines.
Insisted the meanings of words are moulded in our own
minds - basically a matter of choice, and developing
pari passu with the content of the individual's thought.

OLGIATI, Don Francesco (1886-1962). Professor at the
Catholic University of Milan. Worked in collaboration
with Padre Gemelli. Taught history of philosophy and
philosophy of law.

PELAGIUS (born c.360). Early British Christian.
Probably emerged from one of the monasteries in Scot-
land or Ireland. On getting to Rome was staggered by
depths of corruption. Was told this was due to weakness

of human nature. His unorthodox views, taken up more vigorously by his more argumentative followers Coelestius and Julianus, included the idea that people are free to decide and make moral choices. A lot of rest of life spent hearing his views arraigned by Synods and church courts (his greatest opponent was St. Augustine). Favourite maxim - 'If I ought, I can'. He asserted that human beings can make the right moral choices even without the intervention of God.

SARPI, Pietro, later changed name to Paolo (Paulus Servita) (1552-1623). Italian historian and statesman. Prominent member of Servite Order. Became its pro-curator general (1585-8), but came under fire from Inquisition because of his contacts with Protestant leaders. In a quarrel between Pope Paul V and the City of Venice (1606) on a matter of ecclesiastical authority, Sarpi was a passionate defender of the cause of Venice. Was summoned to Rome to account for his conduct. Ecclesiastical enemies tried to have him assassinated in 1607.

Sarpi's chief literary work was Istoria del Concilio Tridentino (History of the Council of Trent). A man skilled in many arts and sciences - expert in canon law and anatomy (seems to have discovered the valves which help the circulation of blood). Istoria del Concilio Tridentino was published in London in 1619 after MS had been taken there by Sir Henry Wootton, British Resident at Venice and personal friend of Sarpi. The flavour is anti-Vatican, almost rationalist and the Jesuit Cardinal Pallavicino brought out a huge tome to answer it.

SUAREZ, Francisco (1548-1617). Spanish Jesuit. Extra-ordinarily prolific Scholastic. Followed the opinions of St. Thomas 'unless he saw good reason not to'. Only twenty out of 1120 opinions diverge from Thomas's. Spared no effort to boost the role of Mary in Catholicism.

SYLLOGISM. One of the figures in formal logic. Always

consists of three assertions in strict logical connection
with each other. Here is a model of the syllogism
Barbara (the model is Aristotle's):-

> MAJOR PREMISS: If all Greeks are Europeans
> MINOR PREMISS: And if all Athenians are Greeks
> CONCLUSION: Then all Athenians are Europeans

TAPARELLI D'AZEGLIO, Padre Luigi (1793-1862).
Neo-Scholastic. As the Vatican Enciclopedia Cattolica
puts it, 'conducted a vigorous campaign for the restoration
of Scholastic philosophy, which had been languishing in
almost universal neglect for about 100 years.' His
restoration work included equally 'vigorous' efforts to
huff and puff some life into natural law. His support of
natural law worked in a reactionary Catholic direction,
to put some philosophical muscle into retrograde doctrines
like the divine origin of authority and authority's right to
persecute unorthodox opinions.

TEILHARD de CHARDIN, Pierre (1881-1955). Palaeon-
tologist. Became Jesuit at eighteen. Soon became
deeply interested in philosophy of Bergson. Tried to
show evolutionism was compatible with Christianity.
Met with steady hostility from superiors. Expelled from
Catholic Institute in 1926. Was 'exiled' to China till 1946.
Took part in palaeontological research which led to dis-
covery of Peking man.
    Consistently attempted to 'reconcile' science and
Catholicism. Main ideas appear in The Phenomenon of
Man, New York, 1959. Some readers seemed impressed
by his kindly, well-meaning nature and charming smile.
But as a philosophical structure his ideas were irreparably
mauled by the biologist Prof. P.B. Medawar (see The
Art of the Soluble, Methuen, London, 1967). For samples
of attacks on Teilhard as unorthodox, see Jacques Maritain,
Le Paysan de la Garonne, Desclée de Brouwer, Paris,
1966, pp.173 ff.

THIASOS (Greek word, probably derived from theos -

God). Religious gathering under the aegis of a God, specially Dionysus. Ended in rowdy procession, with songs, dances and unrestrained yells.

ZHDANOV (1896-1948). Famous as persecutor of any form of non-orthodox art and thought; was a Russian Torquemada in the cultural field under Stalin.

### Footnote

1. Some of his exploits, though (burying populations alive) were too much for the strong stomachs of the Church authorities, and he ended up in prison after innumerable charges had been levelled at him.

FRANCO CORDERO is a Professor of Criminal Procedure at the Catholic University of Milan, although Cardinal Garrone of the Sacra Congregatio pro Institutione Catholica has forbidden him to lecture there. This case has not yet been allowed to come before the Italian High Council for Education, the supreme authority in such matters.

MONSIGNOR CARLO COLOMBO has been director of the Venegono Seminary for many years. He was appointed bishop by Pope Paul VI and is now his theological adviser. His role as guardian of orthodoxy has been officially confirmed by his appointment as Chairman of the Council for the Doctrine of the Faith in the permanent Italian Episcopal Conference. He is also President of the Toniolo Institute of Higher Studies, the financial organisation which controls the Catholic University of Milan.

CARDINAL GABRIELE MARIA GARRONE is responsible for running the Congregation for Catholic Education. He is French and was once considered to belong to the progressive wing of the Roman Curia.

# INDEX

## A
Abelard, 48, 91, 129
Accidents (Scholastic), 36, 71, 72
Adam, 45, 77
Adam and Eve, 60, 71, 76-8
Alacoque, St. Marguerite Marie, 60, 71, 90, 91, 128
Alexandrian School of Philosophy, 45
Anselm, St., 67, 70
Anthropos, myth of, 45
Antigone, 30
Apocalypse, The, 41, 52
Apostles, 50-2, 55
Aquinas, St. Thomas, 25, 36, 42, 54, 56, 62, 63, 70,
        75, 113
Arabs, The, 61
Aristotle, 62, 103, 135
Arius, 47
Arnaldo da Brescia, 98
Astrid, Queen of Belgium, 52
Athanasius, 47
Athis, 73
Averroists, 75, 128

## B
Baptists, 92
Basil, St., 75, 130
Bellarmino, Cardinal, 21, 130
Bernard, St., 91, 92
Binding Efficiency of Law, 30, 31
Bonaiuti, Professor Ernesto, 99, 106, 107
Bosch, Hieronymous, 89
Bougre, Robert le, 80, 129
Bráhman, 46
Bruno, Giordano, 98

## C
Calvin, 42, 90

Carnap, Rudolf, 98
Catholic University of Milan (Università Cattolica
        di Milano), 8, 20-2, 83, 99, 106, 108, 118, 130
China, 62
Christ, 36, 44, 46-9, 54, 55, 71, 72, 74, 81
Church Fathers, 77
Clovis, 85
Cluny, Abbey of, 92
Colombo, Monsignor Carlo, 8, 17, 30, 36, 37, 50-2, 56,
        64, 65, 68-72, 76-8, 84, 99, 100, 103, 137
Communion, The (Holy), 53-7
Constantine, Emperor, 47, 48
Constantinople, Council of, 48
Copernicus, 40
Corinthians, Epistle to, 31, 66
Council of Trent, 19, 49, 53, 70, 77
Counter-Reformation, 30, 42


        D
Darwin, 40, 75
David, Max, 43
De Maistre, 100
Demeter, 73
Dionysus, 73
Drugs, 54


        E
Eckhardt, Meister, 90
Erasmus, 97
Euclid, 44
Eusebius of Nicomedia, 47
Evolution, Theory of, 76-8


        F
Faith, Concept of, 70-3
French Revolution, 82
Freud, 25, 39, 75, 83, 116


        G
Galileo, 40, 76, 79, 98, 102, 106, 107

Gemelli, Father, 22, 78-83, 90, 98, 115, 117, 130, 133
Genesis, 41, 52, 76
Gentile Giovanni, 99
Giannone, 98, 131
Gilson, Etienne, 98, 131
Gli osservanti, 8, 9, 59, 68, 69, 75, 99, 102, 106, 108,
     109, 113-5, 119, 125
Good, The, 35
Gribaldi, Mofa, 96
Guitton, Jean, 75
Guyon, Mme., 39, 125, 131


      H
Hegel, 35, 75, 131
Hobbes, 25
Holy Court (or Holy Office) 79, 102, 103
Holy Mother Church, 51, 74, 77, 89, 92, 96-8, 101, 103,
     104
Holy Spirit (Holy Ghost), 46, 50, 56, 77
Homousios, 47, 48
Humanae Vitae, encyclical by Paul VI, 19, 30
Hume, David, 42, 71
Hypostasis, 47


      I
Id, 88
Immortal Soul, 34
Index (of Prohibited Books), 60
Innocent II, 91
Isis, 73


      J
Jews, The, 61, 81, 115
John, St., (Gospel of), 46, 54


      K
Kelsen, Hans, 98, 132
Kepler, 40
Klein, Melanie, 25, 132

L

Lateran Concordat, 99, 107, 111
Lévy-Bruhl, 36
Logos, 45-9
Logroño, 81
Lombard, Peter (Pietro Lombardo), 53, 109, 132
Loreto, 71
Louis VII, 91
Luther, Martin, 42, 66, 67, 90
Lysenko, 25, 132

M

Magic, 53-7, 117
Magisterium (leading authorities in the Church), 50, 51
    76, 77
Mana, 32, 46, 55, 57
Maranatha!, 45
Marlowe, Christopher, 54
Mary St. (or the Madonna), 51, 52, 70, 71, 91
Marx, Karl, 40, 75
Mauss, M., 57, 117
Medievalism, 78, 82
Mennonites, 92
Messiah, the, 44, 54
Miracles, 80
Mithra, 73
Momigliano, Felice, 81, 115

N

Nietzsche, Friedrich, 25, 116, 133
Nicea, Council of, 47-9
Nicene Creed, 47
Neo-Scholasticism, 70

O

O (in Histoire d'O), 91
Occam (or Ockham), William, 35, 42, 68, 98, 109, 133
Odysseus, 32
Olgiati, Don, 22, 131, 133
Ontological proofs, 67, 70

Orenda, 46
Origen, 47, 49
Orpheus, 45, 73
Orthodoxy, 38-40, 77
Orwell, George, 25
Osius of Cordoba, 47


P
Paraclete (Holy Spirit as ) 46
Paul VI, 19, 30, 45, 46, 124 124
Paul, St., 31, 66, 67
Pelagian indeterminism, 42
Personae, 46, 48
Peter the Venerable, 92
Pharaoh (against Moses and Jews), 57
Phenomenology, 29, 38, 48, 49
Philo of Alexandria, 49
Phoenician towns, 53
Pius IX, 80
Pius XII, 76, 100, 101
Plato, 32, 35, 61, 133
Ptolemaic system, 75, 103
Ptolemies of Egypt, 45


R
Reformation, The, 57
Renaissance, 79, 98
Rimini, Council of, 47-9
Rivista di filosofia neoscolastica, 84
Roman Curia, 92
Ruffini, Cardinal E., 100


S
Sabellian heresy, 47
Sacred Heart, Cult of, 60, 90, 99
Sade, Marquis de, 25
Sarpi, Paolo, 98, 134
Scholastic forms, 35, 42
Scholasticism, 24, 62-5, 67, 70, 79, 103
Sciacca, M.F., 40, 43

Scotists, 23
Scriptures, The (Holy), 50-2, 77, 78
Seleucia, Council of, 47-9
Sophists, 24, 25
Spinoza, 25
Suarez, 70, 134
Substance (Scholastic term), 71, 72
Summa Theologiae, 75
Super-Ego, 88
Syllabus of Errors, 80
Syllogism, 67, 134


T

Taparelli D'Azeglio, Father, 98, 135
Teilhard de Chardin, 76, 135
Tempier Etienne, Bishop of Paris, 62, 63
Tennis Court Oath, 98, 104
Teresa, St., 91
Teutonicus, Johannes, 55
Theodosius, 48
Thiasos, 46
Thomas Aquinas, St., 25, 36, 42, 54, 56, 62, 63, 70,
    75, 113
Thomists, 23
Thomist synthesis, 62, 63
Torquemada, 39, 136
Transubstantiation, 36, 71, 72
Trent, Council of, 19, 49, 53, 70, 77
Trieste University, 21
Trinity, The (Holy), 46-8, 56, 70


U

Ulysses (Odysseus), 32
Università Cattolica di Milano (Catholic University of
    Milan), 8, 20-2, 83, 99, 106, 108, 118, 130


V

Valla, Lorenzo (Italian philologist), 48
Vatican Council, 77

Vita e pensiero (Life and Thought), Italian review, 78, 81, 84, 131

**W**
Way of the Cross (Via Crucis), 34
Whitehead, Alfred North, 68

**Z**
Zhdanov, 25, 136
Zwingli, 53